Table

Leçon 9 135

Leçon 10 151

Leçon 8 119

Leçon 11 169

Fourth Edition

THE FRENCH WORKSHOP

Todd Straus

Kendall Hunt
publishing company

Cover courtesy Ginny Laughlin.
© Interior images Shutterstock, Inc. and Art Explosion: 2, 4, 13, 18, 20, 31, 34, 36, 49, 52, 54, 68, 70, 84, 87, 102, 105, 120, 123, 136, 152, 155, 167, 170, 190, 193, 208, 211, 226, 230, 243, 246, 247

www.kendallhunt.com
Send all inquiries to:
4050 Westmark Drive
Dubuque, IA 52004-1840

Copyright © 2011, 2012, 2013, 2018 by Todd Straus

ISBN 978-1-5249-4911-2

Published in the United States of America

Merci

Thank you to Dr. Frank Forcier at Kendall Hunt for offering me the opportunity to create the two volumes of The French Workshop. I am indebted to Linda Chapman and Charmayne McMurray, my able Project Coordinators. My affectionate appreciation goes to Ginny Laughlin who created the playful cover art. I benefited from a stimulating exchange of ideas with my brilliant and generous Santa Rosa colleague, Terri Frongia. Thanks also to my very willing first-year French students, my guinea pigs.

Finally, I would like to acknowledge Santa Rosa Junior College, where I have taught since 1996. I had previously been employed at a number of reputatious four-year colleges, but it was not until landing at SRJC that I found myself at an institution where excellence of instruction in the undergraduate classroom was duly recognized, supported, honored.

Leçon 1

une calculatrice	un crayon	un ordinateur	un(e) élève
une chaise	une table	un stylo	une porte
une page	des devoirs (masc.)	un sac à dos	un téléphone
une fenêtre des rideaux (masc.)	une place	un professeur un tableau	une carte
un mur	une photo	un mot	un livre

Usage Card no. 1 L'alphabet

Repeat the alphabet several times after your instructor.

A	D	G	J	M	P	S	V	Y
B	E	H	K	N	Q	T	W	Z
C	F	I	L	O	R	U	X	

Usage Drill

Alternating with a partner, say the following letters.

A F D M G T J R M S P E S Z U C Y K H X G
B Q E R H U K X N Y Q S T P W J Z W U R V
C N F L I J L T O V R W U G X K H I O L J

Usage Card no. 2 a (an) = un, une   some = des

un stylo, un mur (use "un" because **stylo** and **mur** are masculine nouns)

une calculatrice, une fenêtre (use "une" because **calculatrice** and **fenêtre** are feminine nouns)

des devoirs, des rideaux (use "des" because **devoirs** and **rideaux** are plural)

Usage Drills

A. Identify items on p. 2 as masculine or feminine.

B. Turn to page 4. Using **un, une** or **des**, name two items on the page that are separated by one other item. Your partner will name the item that sits in between using **un, une** or **des**.

Usage Card no. 3 Numbers 1–10

Repeat these numbers several times after your instructor.

1 = un		6 = six
2 = deux		7 = sept
3 = trois		8 = huit
4 = quatre		9 = neuf
5 = cinq		10 = dix

Usage Drill

Say these numbers in French. (You say the first number, your partner will say the second one, you say the third, etc.)

1, 2, 3, 4, 5, 6, 7, 8, 9, 1, 3, 5, 7, 9, 2, 4, 6, 8, 10, 9, 8, 7, 6, 5, 4, 3, 2, 1
9, 8, 7, 6, 5, 4, 3, 2, 1, 10, 8, 6, 4, 2, 9, 7, 5, 3, 1, 3, 5, 7, 9, 10, 8, 6, 5, 4
4, 7, 1, 2, 8, 10, 9, 4, 2, 1, 7, 6, 5, 3, 9, 8, 10, 3, 6, 4, 9, 6, 3, 1, 4, 7, 6, 2
1, 9, 8, 3, 5, 9, 8, 10, 6, 4, 5, 2, 1, 7, 6, 4, 8, 3, 9, 5, 1, 4, 10, 6, 5, 3, 7, 8

(A, B, C, D)	(E, F, G)	(H, I, J, K)	(L, M, N, O, P)
(Q, R, S, T, U, V)	(W, X, Y, Z)	(1, 2, 3, 4, 5)	(6, 7, 8, 9, 10)
(A, 1, B, 2, C, 3)	(4, D, 5, E, 6, F)	(G, I, 7, J, K, 8)	(9, L, 10, M, P)
(Z, Y, X, W, V)	(E, I, U, O, A)	(10, X, V, 6, 1)	(P, O, R, T, E)
(U, A, E, I, O, U)	(C, R, A, Y, O, N)	(A, E, I, O, U, Y)	(10, 3, 5, J, G)

Conversation 1

Personne 1:	Personne 2:	
Bonjour.		*Hello.*
	Salut.	*Hi.*
Comment allez-vous?		*How are you?*
	Bien, merci. Et vous?	*Fine, thanks. And you?*
Ça va.		*Good.*
	Comment vous appelez-vous?	*What's your name?*
Je m'appelle Dominique*. Et vous?		*My name is Dominique*. And you?*
	Je m'appelle Claude*.	*My name is Claude*.*
Au revoir.		*Good bye.*
	A bientôt.	*See you soon.*

Dominique and Claude are both male and female names in French.

Pratique de la conversation

1. Repeat each line of the Conversation multiple times after your instructor.

2. Practice the whole Conversation several times with a partner.

3. Cover up all the French and try repeating the whole Conversation twice using the English as your guide.

Guide de la prononciation

1. Pronounce these words from the Conversation: all<u>ez</u>, appel<u>ez</u>. How is the [ez] ending pronounced?

2. Pronounce these words: <u>au</u> revoir, Cl<u>au</u>de. How is [au] pronounced?

3. Pronounce: b<u>ien</u>, b<u>ien</u>tôt de r<u>ien</u>. How is [ien] pronounced?

4. Pronounce ç<u>a</u>, v<u>a</u>, s<u>a</u>lut, <u>a</u>ppelle, <u>à</u> bientôt. How is [a] pronounced?

5. Pronounce: v<u>ous</u>, bonj<u>ou</u>r. How is [ou] pronounced?

6. Pronounce: all<u>ez</u>, <u>au</u> revoir, b<u>ien</u>, <u>a</u>ppelle, v<u>ous</u>, appel<u>ez</u>, b<u>ien</u>tôt, s<u>a</u>lut, Cl<u>au</u>de, bonj<u>ou</u>r.

Nom _____

Exercices   Leçon 1

Exercice 1.1 (p. 2) Classification. Write each item given below in an appropriate column.

Small or Light Things	Large or Heavy Things	People	Other

une calculatrice	un crayon	un ordinateur	un tableau	un livre
un élève	une chaise	une table	une photo	un mur
un stylo	une porte	une page	une carte	un professeur
une élève	un sac à dos	un téléphone	un mot	une place
une fenêtre	des devoirs	des rideaux		

Exercice 1.2 (p. 2) Pairs. Create a natural pair from the words in Exercise 1.1.

Example: une carte et* <u>un mur</u>

1. une calculatrice et _____
2. un stylo et _____
3. un élève et _____
4. une fenêtre et _____
5. un tableau et _____
6. une photo et _____
7. un crayon et _____
8. une page et _____
9. un professeur et _____
10. une chaise et _____
11. une porte et _____
12. un sac à dos et _____
13. une place et _____
14. un mot et _____
15. un ordinateur et _____
16. une table et _____
17. un téléphone et _____
18. un livre et _____

*et = and

(p. 2) Rewrite each item adding **un**, **une** or **des**.

Example: livre → <u>un livre</u>

1 ordinateur → _____
2 crayon → _____
3 table → _____
4 porte → _____
5 page → _____
6 fenêtre → _____
7 devoirs → _____
8 tableau → _____
9 stylo → _____

10 calculatrice → _____
11 téléphone → _____
12 élève → _____
13 mot → _____
14 photo → _____
15 mur → _____
16 carte → _____
17 rideaux → _____
18 sac à dos → _____

Exercice de conversation 1.4 (p. 5) Reconstruct Conversation 1 by writing the following sentences in the correct order.

A bientôt.   Bien, merci. Et vous?   Ça va.

Salut.   Je m'appelle Dominique. Et vous?   Comment allez-vous?

Au revoir.   Je m'appelle Claude.   Comment vous appelez-vous?

Personne 1: Bonjour.

Personne 2:

Personne 1:

Personne 2:

Personne 1:

Personne 2:

Personne 1:

Personne 2:

Personne 1:

Personne 2:

Exercice 1.5 (p. 2) Spelling. Complete each word by adding the missing letters.

une c___lc___l___tr___c e   des r___d_____x
un cr___y___n   un t___l___ph___ne

un o___i n___t___r   une f___n___tr___
un é___ve   une pl___ce
une ch___se   un ta___ea___
une t___bl___   une c___r___e
un st___l___   un m___r
une p___rte   une ph___t___
une p___ge   un l___vr___
un s___c à d___s   un pro_____eur

Exercice de conversation 1.6 (p. 5) Fill in the missing words. When you have finished, correct yourself in a different color by turning to p. 5.

Personne 1:   **Personne 2:**

Bonjour.

_____.

Comment allez-_____?

Bien, _____. Et vous?

Ça va.

_____ vous appelez-vous?

Je m'appelle Dominique. _____ vous?

Je m'appelle Claude.

Au _____.

_____ bientôt.

Exercice 1.7 (p. 3) Numbers 1–10. Write out each arithmetic problem.

Example: 1 + 3 = 4   un + trois = quatre

2 + 7 = 9 _____

5 + 3 = 8 _____

4 + 6 = 10 _____

5 + 1 = 6 _____

7 + 2 = 9 _____

3 + 1 = 4 _____

4 + 2 = 6 _____

10 - 5 = 5 _____

8 - 6 = 2 _____

6 + 1 = 7 _____

1 + 7 = 8 _____

4 + 3 = 7 _____

9 − 3 = 6 _____

Exercice de conversation 1.8 Write the French conversation by translating the English. When you have finished, correct yourself in a different color by turning to p. 5.

Personne 1:   **Personne 2:**

_____   *Hello.*

                    _____   *Hi.*

_____   *How are you?*

                    _____   *Fine, thanks. And you?*

_____   *Good.*

                    _____   *What's your name?*

_____   *My name is Dominique. And you?*

                    _____   *My name is Claude.*

_____   *Goodbye.*

                    _____   *See you soon.*

Exercice de composition 1.9 (p. 2) Where might you typically find each of the pictured items in this lesson? (NOTE: on = "sur", in = "dans", under = "sous" and "avec" = with.

Example: une table: <u>sous des livres</u> (under some books)

_____

_____

_____

_____

_____

_____

_____

For additional practice, please access [1] youtube.com. Search: "Todd Straus The French Workshop Level 1" and [2] quizlet.com. Search: "TFW Level 1".

Question/Réponse 1

Cover up the **Réponses typiques** below. Then, alternating with a partner, ask and answer the following questions. Glance at the **Réponses typiques** when you need guidance. (Note: There is more than one way to answer some questions correctly.)

Questions

1. Salut. Ça va?
2. Bonjour. Comment allez-vous?
3. Comment vous appelez-vous?
4. Je m'appelle Dominique. Et vous?
5. Au revoir, Claude.
6. Bien, merci. Et vous?
7. A bientôt.
8. Un plus quatre?
9. Trois plus six?
10. Deux plus cinq?
11. Cinq plus trois?
12. Six plus quatre?

Réponses typiques

1. Bonjour. Bien, merci.
2. Ça va.
3. Je m'appelle Dominique. Et vous?
4. Je m'appelle Claude.
5. Au revoir. A bientôt.
6. Ça va.
7. Au revoir.
8. Un plus quatre font cinq
9. Trois plus six font neuf.
10. Deux plus cinq font sept.
11. Cinq plus trois font huit.
12. Six plus quatre font dix.

Name _____

Histoire/Géographie 1

A. French school children learn to draw France as a hexagon, a six-sided figure. In fact, the French often refer to their country as "L'hexagone".

LA FRANCE

B. Online Search.

1 Add and label the three most populated French cities on the map of France above.

2 Label (in French) the Atlantic Ocean, the Mediterranean Sea and the English Channel.

3 What is the population of France? _____ And the population of your native country? _____

4 Is the area of France larger than, smaller than, or about the same size as Texas?
_____

5 What is the distance in kilometers between San Francisco and New York?
_____

What is the distance in kilometers between New York and Paris?
_____

6 Which countries share a border with France? (Write their names in French.)
_____

The Gender of Words in French

If a word ends with the letters e **or** on, **guess** feminine.

If a word ends in any letter other than e or on, **guess** masculine.

EXCEPTIONS:

EXCEPTIONS:

un livre

    une photo

Each time you learn vocabulary from a new Picture Page, you will list the EXCEPTIONS. This way, you will only have to memorize the gender of the words on this page.

Leçon

2

un dictionnaire

un examen

un problème

une horloge

une salle de classe

un étudiant

une étudiante

une personne

une chose

une question

une réponse

un sol

une lumière

une leçon

une vidéo

un DVD

une corbeille à papier

une montre

un parapluie

une liste

Usage Card no. 4 Numbers 11–20

11 = onze	13 = treize	15 = quinze	17 = dix-sept	19 = dix-neuf
12 = douze	14 = quatorze	16 = seize	18 = dix-huit	20 = vingt

Usage Drill

Alternating with a partner, say the following numbers.

1, 2, 3, 4, 5, 6, 7, 8, 9, 10, 11, 12, 13, 14, 15, 16, 17, 18, 19, 20, 19, 18, 17, 16, 15, 14, 13, 12, 11, 10
20, 1, 19, 2, 18, 3, 17, 4, 16, 5, 15, 6, 14, 7, 13, 8, 12, 9, 11, 10, 9, 11, 8, 12, 7, 13, 6, 14, 5, 11, 6, 1
19, 4, 16, 6, 13, 1, 17, 15, 2, 12, 11, 13, 12, 14, 5, 4, 3, 6, 16, 19, 9, 8, 7, 17, 15, 10, 3, 12, 9, 14, 13

Usage Card no. 5 Articles

a = un, une	un livre (masc.), une porte (fem.)
the = le, la, l', les	le livre (masc.), la porte (fem.), l'élève (starts with a vowel), les murs (plural), les films (plural), les étudiants (plural)
some = des	des tables

Usage Drills

Translate these phrases from French to English and English to French.

A. des murs, un dictionnaire, une place, le professeur, l'horloge, un tableau. les photos, des sacs à dos, le stylo, des livres, la photo, une table, les horloges, l'ordinateur

B. the word, a book, the telephones, the door, a computer, some pencils, the calculator, a seat, some windows, the wall, a word, some pages, the floors, the floor, a floor, some floors

Usage Card no. 6 11 Prépositions

Here are some useful prepositions that indicate where things are:

on = sur	on a table = sur une table
under = sous	under the book = sous le livre
in = dans	in the dictionary = dans le dictionnaire
between, in between = entre	between the videos = entre les vidéos
in front of = devant	in front of the door = devant la porte
behind = derrière	behind the desk = derrière le bureau
avec = with	with a pen = avec un stylo
above = au-dessus de*	above a student = au-dessus d'un élève
near = près de*	near a wall = près d'un mur
far from = loin de*	far from Thomas = loin de Thomas
next to, beside = à côté de *	beside a pencil = à côté d'un crayon

* The word de becomes d' before a word that begins with a vowel or an "h".

Usage Drills

A. <u>Translate these phrases:</u> sous une fenêtre, au-dessus d'un élève, sur une table, à côté d'un stylo, devant le tableau, derrière la porte, entre des rideaux, dans un dictionnaire, loin d'un tableau, près d'une horloge

B. <u>Translate these phrases:</u> above a telephone, under the seat, near a window, above a floor, next to a wall, between the words, under a page, near a clock, far from a classroom, behind the teacher, in front of the board

C. Tell where things are on page 18 using one of the prepositions. (For instance, "à côté d'une leçon".) Your partner will then guess to which item you are referring. ("une vidéo")

(0, 1, 2, 3)

(4, 5, 6, 7)

(8, 9, 10, 11)

(12, 13, 14, 15)

(16, 17, 18, 19)

(20, 18, 16, 14)

(12, 10, 8, 6)

(4, 2, 1, 3)

(5, X, 9, P)

(13, V, J, 15)

(20, E, R, 4)

(18, 14, B, N)

(I, K, H, 8)

(T, U, 14, 16)

(5, C, G, J)

(P, B, A, Y)

(9, 19, 20, W)

(13, 16, Q, K)

(E, I, U, 1)

(4, 13, 18, F)

Conversation 2

Personne 1:	Personne 2:	
Salut, Martine!		*Hi, Martina!*
	Salut, George!	*Hi, George!*
Comment vas-tu?		*How are you doing?*
	Bien, merci. Et toi?	*Fine, thanks. And you?*
Ça va bien!		*Very well.*
	Tu vas où?	*Where are you going?*
Chez moi. Et toi?		*Home. And you?*
	A l'école.	*To school.*
Bon courage!		*Good luck!*
	Merci! Toi aussi!	*Thanks! You too!*
Salut!		*Bye!*
	Ciao!	*Ciao!*

Pratique de la conversation

1. Repeat each line multiple times after your instructor.

2. Practice the whole Conversation multiple times with a partner.

3. Cover up all the French and try repeating the whole Conversation twice using the English as your guide.

Guide de la prononciation

1. Pronounce these words: Salut, tu, une, étudiant and mur. How is [u] pronounced?

2. Pronounce: ou, bonjour, courage and sous. How is [ou] pronounced?

3. Pronounce: salut, vas-tu, à l'école, courage, ciao. How is [a] pronounced?

4. Pronounce: vous, salut, courage, étudiant, bonjour, ciao, tu, vas, lumière, parapluie.

Exercices   Leçon 2

Exercice 2.1 (p. 18) Classification. Write each word given below in one appropriate column.

Things That Feature Words	Heavy Things	People	Other

une étudiante   une chose   une vidéo   des mots   une personne

un dictionnaire   une élève   une corbeille à papier   une lumière   une leçon

une photo   un sac à dos   une place   une porte   un livre

un mur   un DVD   une page   un problème   une table

un sol   un téléphone   une réponse   une horloge   un crayon

un parapluie   une liste   des rideaux   une salle de classe   un examen

une question   une montre   une chaise   une carte   des devoirs

Exercice 2.2 (pp. 2, 18) Pairs. Add a second item to make a natural pair.

Example: un crayon et <u>une liste</u>

1 une étudiante et _____
2 un dictionnaire et _____
3 un mur et _____
4 un sol et _____
5 un parapluie et _____
6 une question et _____
7 un examen et _____
8 un ordinateur et _____
9 une chose et _____
10 une élève et _____
11 un DVD et _____
12 une photo et _____
13 une liste et _____
14 une horloge et _____
15 une table et _____

16 une montre et _____
17 des rideaux et _____
18 une chaise et _____
19 un crayon et _____
20 une réponse et _____
21 des mots et _____
22 une lumière et _____
23 une corbeille à papier et _____
24 une vidéo et _____
25 une porte et _____
26 une salle de classe et _____
27 une leçon et _____
28 un problème et _____
29 une personne et _____
30 des devoirs et _____

Exercice 2.3 (p. 3) Fill in the blank squares below using: un, une, le, la, l', les, des.

a/an	the	the	some
un dictionnaire	dictionnaire	dictionnaires	dictionnaires
porte	porte	les portes	portes
examen	examen	examens	examens
vidéo	le livre	photos	des parapluies
mot	élève	devoirs	crayons
table	page	rideaux	horloges

Exercice 2.4 (p. 18) Spelling. Complete each word by adding the missing letters.

un d___ct___nn___re

une s___ll___ de cl_____e

une ch___se

une qu_____t_____n

une l___m_____re

une c___rb_____lle à p___p_____r

une m___ntr___

un p___r___pl_____

une l___st___

un or_____teur

un st_____o

une v___d___o

une h_____l___g___

un m___r

une p___g___

un cr_____n

une c___lc___l___tr_____

une ch_____s___

un s___l

une r___p___n___e

un pr___bl___me

des d___v_____rs

Exercice de conversation 2.5 (p. 21) Reconstruct Conversation 2 by writing the following sentences in the correct order.

Comment vas-tu? Bon courage! Bien, merci. Et toi?

Merci! Toi aussi! Chez moi. Et toi? Ciao!

A l'école. Salut! Ça va bien!

Salut, George! Tu vas où?

Personne 1: Salut, Martine!

Personne 2:

Personne 1:

Personne 2:

Personne 1:

Personne 2:

Personne 1:

Personne 2:

Personne 1:

Personne 2:

Personne 1:

Personne 2:

Exercice 2.6 (pp. 3, 19) Numbers 1–19. Write out each arithmetic problem.

Example: 4 x 2 = 8   quatre x deux = huit

1 + 5 = 6   _____

9 x 2 = 18   _____

19 – 13 = 6 _____

4 x 3 = 12   _____

9 + 8 = 17   _____

6 x 3 = 18   _____

6 + 14 = 20 _____

7 + 2 = 9   _____

10 – 8 = 2   _____

11 + 6 = 17 _____

16 + 2 = 18 _____

3 x 5 = 15   _____

Exercice 2.7 (p. 19) Où? Write where each thing would usually be. Use: **sous, sur, dans, entre, au-dessus de/d', devant, derrière, à côté de/d', près de/d', loin de.**

Example: un livre <u>dans</u> un sac à dos

1 un professeur _____ un tableau

2 une carte _____ une personne

3 une photo _____ un livre

4 des stylos _____ un sac à dos

5 une porte _____ une personne

6 une étudiante _____ deux étudiants

7 un(e) élève _____ une salle de classe

8 un DVD _____ une table

9 une corbeille à papier _____ une porte

10 une chose _____ une corbeille à papier

11 une calculatrice _____ un problème d'arithmétique

12 un sol _____ une place

13 une réponse _____ un livre

14 un examen _____ un(e) élève

15 un problème _____ une page

16 un sol _____ des murs

17 un mur _____ une corbeille à papier

18 une lumière _____ un élève

19 un parapluie _____ une personne

20 une liste _____ un téléphone

Exercice de conversation 2.8 Fill in the missing words. When you have finished, correct yourself in a different color by turning to p. 21.

Personne 1:

Salut, Martine!

Comment_____-tu?

Ça va _____ !

Chez _____. Et toi?

_____ courage!

Salut!

Personne 2:

Salut, George!

Bien, _____. Et toi?

Tu vas _____

A l'_____.

Merci! Toi _____!

_____!

Write the French conversation by translating the English. When you are finished, correct yourself in a different color by turning to p. 21.

Personne 1:   **Personne 2:**

_____

                              _____

_____   *Hi, Martina!*

                              _____   *Hi, George!*

_____   *How are you doing?*

                              _____   *Fine, thanks. And you?*

_____   *Very well.*

                              _____   *Where are you going?*

_____   *Home. And you?*

                              _____   *To school.*

_____   *Good luck!*

                              _____   *Thanks! You too!*

_____   *Bye!*

                              _____   *Ciao!*

Describe where at your place of residence 10 items are located in relation to other items. Use all 11 prepositions (see p. 19).

Example: <u>La carte est sur le mur.</u> [NOTE: "is" = est; "are" = sont.]

_____

_____

_____

_____

_____

_____

_____

_____

_____

_____

For additional practice, please access [1] youtube.com. Search: "Todd Straus The French Workshop Level 1" and [2] quizlet.com. Search: "TFW Level 1".

Question/Réponse 2

Cover up the **Réponses typiques** below. Then, alternating with a partner, ask and answer the following questions. Glance at the **Réponses typiques** when you need guidance. (Note: There is more than one way to answer some questions correctly.)

Questions

1. Deux plus cinq?
2. Quatre plus six?
3. Huit plus un?
4. Trois plus huit?
5. Neuf plus sept?
6. Onze plus trois?
7. Quatre plus quatorze?
8. Douze plus cinq?
9. Un plus quinze?
10. Dix-neuf plus un?

11. C'est normal ou pas normal: un mot dans un dictionnaire?
12. Normal ou pas normal: un parapluie au-dessus d'une personne?
13. Normal ou pas normal: un sol sur une montre?
14. Normal ou pas normal: une liste dans une lumière?
15. Normal ou pas normal: une horloge dans une salle de classe?
16. Normal ou pas normal: une corbeille à papier près d'un mur?
17. Normal ou pas normal: une chaise dans une carte?
18. Normal ou pas normal: des pages dans un livre?
19. Normal ou pas normal: un mot sous un ordinateur?
20. Normal ou pas normal: une fenêtre derrière des rideaux?

Réponses typiques

1. Deux plus cinq font sept.
2. Quatre plus six font dix.
3. Huit plus un font neuf.
4. Trois plus huit font onze.
5. Neuf plus sept font seize.
6. Onze plus trois font quatorze.
7. Quatre plus quatorze font dix-huit.
8. Douze plus cinq font dix-sept.
9. Un plus quinze font seize.
10. Dix-neuf plus un font vingt.

11. C'est normal.
12. C'est normal.
13. Ce n'est pas normal.
14. Ce n'est pas normal.
15. C'est normal.
16. C'est normal.
17. Ce n'est pas normal.
18. C'est normal.
19. Ce n'est pas normal.
20. C'est normal.

Name _____

Histoire/Géographie 2

A. Label (in French) The Atlantic Ocean, The English Channel and The Mediterranean Sea. Place the three largest French cities on the map.

LA FRANCE

B. Online Search.

1 Add the next four largest French cities to the map.

2 Label (en français) Spain, Italy, Switzerland, Germany, Belgium and Luxemburg in their approximate locations.

3 What is the T.G.V.? _____

How long does it take to go from Paris to Bordeaux on the T.G.V.? _____

What is the maximum speed of the T.G.V.? _____ How much will

a second class ticket from Paris to Bordeaux cost? _____ How much

is that in your currency? _____

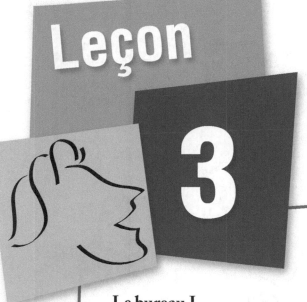

Leçon 3

un bureau

un tableau d'affichage

un bureau

une tasse

un clavier

une souris

une feuille de papier

un laptop

un trombone

un tiroir

une bouteille

un écran

un fauteuil

un(e) patron/nne

un(e) employé(e)

un(e) secrétaire

un(e) collègue

un placard

une clé

un agenda

Usage Card no. 7 What's this? = Qu'est-ce que c'est?

Pronounce the following conversation several times with a partner. Insert the name of a different page 34 item each time in the blank.

PERS 1: **Bonjour. Ça va?**   *Hello. How's it going?*

PERS 2: **Ça va bien.**   *Great.*

PERS 1: (pointing at an item) **Qu'est-ce que c'est?**   *What's this?*

PERS 2: **C'est un(e) _____. / Ce sont des _____s.**   *It's a _____. /*
                                                      They're _____s.

PERS 1: **Merci beaucoup.**   *Thank you very much.*

PERS 2: **De rien.**   *Sure.*

Usage Card no. 8 this, these

To express **"this"** before a noun, use
ce (before a masc. noun)
cet (before a masc. noun that starts with a vowel)
cette (before a fem. noun)
To express **"these"** before a noun, use
ces

Usage Drill

A. Translate these phrases. 1. cette photo 2. ces mots 3. ce livre 4. ces cartes
5. ce sac à dos 6. ce tableau 7. ces téléphones 8. cet élève 9. cet ordinateur 10. ces crayons

B. Translate these phrases. 1. this appointment book 2. this laptop 3. these paperclips
4. these screens 5. this cup 6. this problem 7. this answer 8. this word

---

Usage Card no. 9 I love, I like, I hate

J'adore (I love)
J'aime bien (I like)
Je déteste (I hate)

Usage Drill

Say how you feel about the following things. Your partner will feel differently about each one.

1 le placard   3 ces mots   5 les clés   7 cet ordinateur

2 la page   4 cet agenda   6 la souris   8 ce tiroir

(1, 2, 3, 4, 5)

(6, 7, 8, 9, 10)

(11, 12, 13, 14, 15)

(16, 17, 18, 19, 20)

(A, B, C, D, E)

(F, G, H, I, J)

(K, L, M, N, O)

(P, Q, R, S, T)

(U, V, W, X, Y, Z)

(B, 18, Q, 7, K)

(9, 20, T, 13, U)

(7, 15, D, V, E)

(16, P, U, I, 8)

(6, 18, A, F, J)

(G, 1, N, X, Z)

(Z, 12, B, H, K)

(15, C, Y, E, I)

(U, D, I, J, G)

(13, 16, W, E, R)

(2, 11, Q, U, 3)

Conversation 3

Personne 1:	Personne 2:		
Bonjour, monsieur.		*Hello, sir.*	
	Bonjour, mademoiselle.		*Hello, miss.*
Excusez-moi de vous déranger.		*Sorry to bother you.*	
	Ce n'est pas grave.		*Don't worry about it.*
Comment ça va?		*How are you?*	
	Pas mal. Et vous?		*Not bad. And you?*
Bien, merci.		*Fine, thanks.*	
	Comment vous appelez-vous?		*What's your name?*
Je m'appelle Claude.		*My name is Claude.*	
	Et moi, je m'appelle Dominique.		*And I'm Dominique.*
Enchanté.		*Glad to meet you.*	
	Vous êtes d'où?		*Where are you from?*
De Paris. Et vous?		*From Paris. And you?*	
	Dc Bruxelles.		*From Brussels.*
Au revoir. A bientôt.		*Bye. See you soon.*	
	Oui. A demain.		*Yes. See you tomorrow.*

Pratique de la conversation

Repeat each line of the Conversation multiple times after your instructor. Then practice the whole Conversation with a partner. Next, cover the French and try repeating the Conversation twice using the English as your guide.

Guide de la prononciation

1 Pronounce: comment, enchanté and déranger. How are [en] and [an] pronounced?

2 Pronounce: excusez, m'appelle, Bruxelles, merci and mademoiselle. How is [e] pronounced when followed by two consonants?

3 Pronounce: moi, au revoir, trois and mademoiselle. How is [oi] pronounced?

4 Pronounce: bonjour, vous, d'où, souris and oui. How is [ou] pronounced?

Exercices   Leçon 3

Exercice 3.1 (pp. 2, 18, 34) Classification. Write each item given below in an appropriate column.

Things We Carry in One Hand	Furniture and Equipment	People	Other

un agenda   une clé   un placard   des devoirs   un secrétaire
un sol   un parapluie   des rideaux   une horloge   un ordinateur
un patron   un employé   un fauteuil   un trombone   un tiroir
une bouteille   un laptop   une feuille de papier   une souris   un clavier
un bureau   un tableau d'affichage   un crayon   une tasse   une réponse
une montre   un examen   une place   une élève   une calculatrice
un mur   un collègue   un tableau   un problème   un DVD

Exercice 3.2 (pp. 2, 18, 34) Pairs. Put each item into a natural pair using French words that you know.

Example: un crayon et <u>une liste</u>

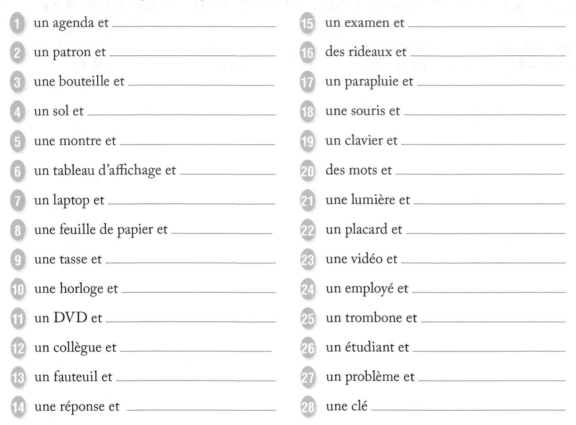

1. un agenda et _____
2. un patron et _____
3. une bouteille et _____
4. un sol et _____
5. une montre et _____
6. un tableau d'affichage et _____
7. un laptop et _____
8. une feuille de papier et _____
9. une tasse et _____
10. une horloge et _____
11. un DVD et _____
12. un collègue et _____
13. un fauteuil et _____
14. une réponse et _____

15. un examen et _____
16. des rideaux et _____
17. un parapluie et _____
18. une souris et _____
19. un clavier et _____
20. des mots et _____
21. une lumière et _____
22. un placard et _____
23. une vidéo et _____
24. un employé et _____
25. un trombone et _____
26. un étudiant et _____
27. un problème et _____
28. une clé _____

Exercice 3.3 (p. 34) Spelling. Complete each word by adding the missing letters.

un ag___nda   une cl___   un pl___c_____d

un c___ll___g_____   un s___cr___t_____re   un p___r___pl_____e

des r___d_____x   une h___rl___ge   un p___tr___n

un e___pl___yé   un f_____te_____l   un tr_____bone

un t___r_____r   une t_____le   un l___pt___p

un cr___y___n   une s_____r___s   un cl___v_____r

un b___r_____u   une t___sse   une r___p___ns___

une m___nt___e   un ex___m_____   une f_____lle de

un t___bl_____ d'aff___ch___ge   p___p _____r

Execice de conversation 3.4 (p. 37) Reconstruct Conversation 3 by writing the following sentences in the correct order.

De Bruxelles.

Vous êtes d'où?

De Paris. Et vous?

Au revoir. A bientôt.

Oui. A demain.

Je m'appelle Claude.

Enchanté.

Et moi, je m'appelle Dominique.

Pas mal. Et vous?

Bonjour, mademoiselle.

Excusez-moi de vous déranger.

Ce n'est pas grave.

Comment ça va?

Bien, merci.

Personne 1: Bonjour, monsieur.

Personne 2:

Personne 1:

Personne 2:

Personne 1:

Personne 2:

Personne 1:

Personne 2: Comment vous appelez-vous?

Personne 1:

Personne 2:

Personne 1:

Personne 2:

Personne 1:

Personne 2:

Personne 1:

Personne 2:

Exercice 3.5 (pp. 3, 19) Numbers 1–20. Write out each arithmetic problem.

Example: 4 x 2 = 8   quatre x deux = huit

1 + 5 = 6   _____

9 x 2 = 18   _____

$18 - 13 = 5$ _____

$4 \times 3 = 12$ _____

$9 + 8 = 17$ _____

$6 \times 3 = 18$ _____

$8 + 12 = 20$ _____

$7 + 2 = 9$ _____

$10 - 8 = 2$ _____

$11 + 3 = 14$ _____

$16 + 2 = 18$ _____

$3 \times 5 = 15$ _____

Exercice 3.6 (p. 19) Où? Write where each item would usually be. Use: **sous, sur, dans, entre, au-dessus de/d', devant, derrière, à côté de/d', près de/d', loin de/d'.**

Example: un livre <u>dans</u> un sac à dos

1. un professeur _____ un tableau

2. une carte _____ un mur

3. une photo _____ une fenêtre

4. des stylos _____ un sac à dos

5. un mur _____ une horloge

6. une leçon _____ un livre

7. un(e) élève _____ la porte

8. un DVD _____ une table

9. une corbeille à papier _____ un mur

10. une chose _____ une corbeille à papier

11. une calculatrice _____ un problème d'arithmétique

12. un sol _____ une place

13 un sac à dos _____ deux fenêtres

14 un examen _____ un(e) élève

15 un problème _____ une page

16 un sol _____ quatre murs

17 un patron _____ deux employés

18 une lumière _____ un élève

19 un parapluie _____ une personne

20 une liste _____ un téléphone

Exercice de conversation 3.7 Fill in the missing words from Conversation 3. When you are done, correct yourself in a different color by turning to p. 37.

Personne 1:

Bonjour, monsieur.

Excusez-moi de _____

Comment _____

Bien, _____.

Je m' _____.

Enchanté.

De Paris. Et _____

Au revoir. A _____

Personne 2:

Bonjour, _____

Ce n'est _____

Pas _____. Et vous?

Comment vous _____

Et moi, _____

Vous êtes _____

De Bruxelles.

Oui. A _____

(pp. 3, 19, 35) Fill in the following chart.

a/an	the	some	this	these
une clé	mur	placards	tiroir	employés
sol	l'agenda	fauteuils	employé	laptops
examen	tasses	des pages	liste	souris
bouteille	rideaux	écrans	cette réponse	horloges
souris	élève	stylos	patronne	ces tiroirs

Exercice de conversation 3.9 Write the French conversation by translating the English. When you're done, correct yourself in a different color by turning to p. 37.

Personne 1: **Personne 2:**

Hello, sir.

Hello, miss.

Sorry to bother you.

Don't worry about it.

How are you?

Not bad. And you?

Fine, thanks.

What's your name?

My name is Claude.

And I'm Dominique.

Glad to meet you.

Where are you from?

From Paris. And you?

From Brussels.

Bye. See you soon.

Yes. See you tomorrow.

Exercice de composition 3.10 How do you like the things in your room? Say which ones you love, like and hate. Include where each thing is. Write ten sentences.

Example: J'adore l'ordinateur sur le bureau.

_____

_____

_____

_____

_____

_____

_____

_____

_____

For additional practice, please access [1] youtube.com. Search: "Todd Straus The French Workshop Level 1" and [2] quizlet.com. Search: "TFW Level 1".

Question/Réponse 3

Cover up the **Réponses typiques** below. Then, alternating with a partner, ask and answer the following questions. Glance at the **Réponses typiques** when you need guidance. (Note: There is more than one way to answer some questions correctly.)

Questions

1. Vingt moins douze?
2. Treize moins sept?
3. Dix-neuf moins deux?
4. Dix-huit moins sept?
5. Seize moins six?
6. Quinze plus cinq?
7. Huit moins sept?
8. Dix-sept moins un?
9. Normal ou pas normal: un trombone dans un tiroir?
10. Normal ou pas normal: un secrétaire sur un tableau d'affichage?
11. Normal ou pas normal: un écran derrière un mur?
12. Normal ou pas normal: un employé dans un fauteuil?
13. Normal ou pas normal: une clé sous un fauteuil?
14. Normal ou pas normal: une souris dans une tasse?
15. Normal ou pas normal: des devoirs dans une bouteille.

Réponses typiques

1. Huit.
2. Six.
3. Dix-sept.
4. Onze.
5. Dix.
6. Vingt.
7. Un
8. Seize.
9. C'est normal.
10. Ce n'est pas normal.
11. Cc n'est pas normal.
12. C'est normal.
13. Ce n'est pas normal.
14. Ce n'est pas normal.
15. Ce n'est pas normal.

Histoire/Géographie 3

A. Outline France as a six-sided figure. Add the seven largest cities as well as the names of three surrounding bodies of water and six neighboring countries. (All in French)

LA FRANCE

B. Online Search.

1 Add Great Britain to your map (en français)

2 Add cities 8 through 10 to your map.

3 Add the Alps and the Pyrenees mountains to your map (en français)

Leçon 4

un cahier

une note

un document

un argent

une lettre

une enveloppe

une imprimante

un message

une réunion

une idée

un calendrier

des toilettes (f.)

une plante verte

un job

une pause café

5 heures

une semaine

une date

une heure

un mois

Usage Card no. 10 Les 7 jours de la semaine

Work Days	Weekend Days
lundi	samedi
mardi	dimanche
mercredi	
jeudi	
vendredi	

Usage Drills

A. Say the following days of the week. (Use the complete French word for each day.)

lun, mar, mer, jeu, ven, sam, dim, sam, ven, jeu, mer, mar, jeu, dim, lun, ven

l ma, me, j, v, s, d, ma, me, v, s, j, l, me, ma, j, s, d, l, ma, v, s, d, j, me, ma

B. Translate each day. (Use the complete French word for each one.)

Mon, Wed, Fri, Tue, Thu, Sun, Sat, Thu, Wed, Mon, Tue, Sun, Wed, Tue, Fri, Sun, Thu, Wed, Mon, Sun, Wed, Tue, Fri, Sun, Thu, Sat, Wed, Tue, Mon, Wed

C. Say each item and then the day or number that immediately precedes it. Alternate with a partner.

Example: mardi…… <u>lundi</u>

1 jeudi
2 six
3 dix-huit
4 quinze
5 dimanche

6 lundi
7 mercredi
8 dix
9 treize
10 dix-sept

11 mardi
12 vendredi
13 samedi
14 trois
15 seize

Usage Card no. 11 there is/are

il y a = there is/are

Examples: Il y a une lampe sur le bureau.

              Il y a des enveloppes dans le tiroir.

Usage Drills

Your roommate is searching for the following items. Say where they are using il y a.

1. une plante verte 2. un document 3. un dictionnaire 4. des réponses 5. une fenêtre 6. un écran
7. une bouteille 8. des dates 9. un tableau 10. des rideaux 11. un job 12. un crayon

(11, 12, Mon)	(16, 15, Tue, 14, 13)	(12, Wed, 13, 14)	(Thu, 16, 11)
(15, 14, Fri, 16)	(Sat, Sun, 13, 16)	(15, 14, 13, 12)	(Mon, Wed, Fri)
(11, 13, Sat, Tue)	(11, 14, 16, Sun)	(19, 18, Wed, Thu)	(18, 19, Tue, Thu)
(19, 18, 17, 16)	(Sun, Sat, Fri, Thu)	(11, 13, 15, 17, 19)	(10, Thu, Sat, Mon)
(19, 18, 17, 16, 15, 14)	(13, 12, 11, 10, 9, 8)	(7, 6, 5, 4, 3, 2, 1, 0)	(Tue, Mon, Sun, Sat)

Conversation 4

Personne 1:	Personne 2:	
Salut.		*Hi.*
	Quoi de neuf?	*What's new?*
Pas beaucoup. Et toi?		*Not much. And you?*
	Rien de spécial.	*Nothing special.*
Tu t'appelles Claude, n'est-ce pas?		*Your name is Claude, right?*
	Moi? Non. Dominique.	*Me? No. Dominique.*
Oh, pardon.		*Oh, sorry.*
	Ce n'est pas grave.	*No problem.*
Tu es de Paris, n'est-ce pas?		*You're from Paris, right?*
	Moi? Non. De Bruxelles.	*Me? No. From Brussels.*
Oh, pardon.		*Oh, sorry.*
	Ce n'est pas grave.	*No problem.*
Eh bien… Salut.		*Well… Bye.*
	Ciao.	*Ciao.*

Pratique de la conversation

Repeat each line of the Conversation multiple times after your instructor. Then practice the whole Conversation with a partner. Next, cover the French and try repeating the Conversation twice using the English as your guide.

Guide de la prononciation

1. Pronounce: vendredi, comment, dimanche calendrier and plante. How are [en] and [an] pronounced?

2. Pronounce: note, enveloppe, sol, job, personne, téléphone and document. How is [o] pronounced?

3. Pronounce: salut, une, mur, calculatrice, étudiant, bureau, Bruxelles. How is [u] pronounced?

4. Pronounce: calendrier, téléphone, tu, dans, entre, école, devant, sur, du, enveloppe, imprimante, parapluie, réunion, document.

Exercices   Leçon 4

Exercice 4.1 (pp. 2, 18, 34, 52) Classification. Write each word given below in an appropriate column.

Associated with Time	Things We Carry in One Hand	People and Furntiure	Other

un agenda
un calendrier
un employé
une pause café
une heure
un mois
une clé
une bouteille

5 heures
des toilettes
une idée
un message
un tableau
   d'affichage
une date
une feuille de
   papier

un patron
un placard
un argent
un fauteuil
une enveloppe
une plante verte
un écran
une collégue

une semaine
une imprimante
des devoirs
une souris
une réunion
un job
une tasse

un secrétaire
un document
un tiroir
un clavier
un cahier
une note
un bureau

Exercice 4.2 (pp. 2, 18, 34, 52) Pairs. Put each word into a natural pair using French words that you know.

Example: un crayon et <u>une liste</u>

1. une date et _____
2. une heure et _____
3. un mois et _____
4. un patron et _____
5. des trombones et _____
6. un tableau d'affichage et _____
7. une clé et _____
8. un argent et _____
9. une tasse et _____
10. une horloge et _____
11. une plante verte et _____
12. un agenda et _____
13. un fauteuil et _____

14. une réunion et _____
15. une note et _____
16. une pause café et _____
17. une enveloppe et _____
18. un clavier et _____
19. un mot et _____
20. une lumière et _____
21. un placard et _____
22. une vidéo et _____
23. des employés et _____
24. un job et _____
25. une semaine et _____
26. une feuille de papier et _____

Exercice 4.3 (pp. 3, 19) Numbers 1–19. Write out each arithmetic problem.

Example: 4 x 2 = 8   <u>quatre x deux = huit</u>

1 + 15 = 16 _____

9 + 2 = 11 _____

18 – 12 = 6 _____

4 x 5 = 20 _____

9 + 4 = 13 _____

8 - 3 = 5 _____

14 + 3 = 17 _____

19 – 9 = 10 _____

6 + 7 = 13 _____

Exercice 4.4 (pp. 2, 18, 34, 52) Write as many French words as you can recall for each category.

People	On a Desk	On the Floor	Associated with Time

Exercice 4.5 (pp. 2, 18, 34, 52) Write three or four things that might be contained in each item.

Example: un calendrier: <u>une photo, des dates, des mois, des semaines</u>

1. un message: _____

2. une semaine: _____

3. une leçon: _____

4. une salle de classe: _____

5. un tiroir: _____

6. un examen: _____

7. un sac à dos: _____

8. une corbeille à papier: _____

Exercice de conversation 4.6 (p. 55) Reconstruct Conversation 4 by writing the following sentences in the correct order.

Quoi de neuf?   Ciao.   Eh bien… Salut.

Ce n'est pas grave.   Oh, pardon.   Moi? Non. De Bruxelles.

Tu es de Paris, n'est-ce pas?   Pas beaucoup. Et toi?   Ce n'est pas grave.

Oh, pardon.   Tu t'appelles Claude, n'est-ce pas?   Rien de special.

Personne 1: Salut.

Personne 2:

Personne 1:

Personne 2:

Personne 1:

Personne 2: Moi? Non. Dominique.

Personne 1:

Personne 2:

Personne 1:

Personne 2:

Personne 1:

Personne 2:

Personne 1:

Personne 2:

Exercice 4.7 (p. 19) Write where each thing would usually be. Use: **sous, sur, dans, entre, au-dessus de/d', devant, derrière, à côté de/d', près de/d', loin de/d'.**

1. une date _____ sur _____ un calendrier

2. des toilettes _____ un bureau

3. une lettre _____ une enveloppe

4. un tableau d'affichage _____ une note

5. une fenêtre _____ des rideaux

6 une porte _____ une fenêtre

7 un document _____ un ordinateur

8 une secrétaire _____ une porte

9 une souris _____ un ordinateur

10 une clé _____ une porte

11 huit heures _____ sept heures et neuf heures

12 un calendrier _____ un mur

13 un sol _____ une place

14 une horloge _____ un bureau

15 un collègue _____ une collègue

Exercice de conversation 4.8 Write the French conversation by translating the English. When you have finished, correct yourself in a different color by turning to p. 55.

Personne 1:   **Personne 2:**

_____

        _____   *Hi.*

        _____   *What's new?*

_____   *Not much. And you?*

        _____   *Nothing special.*

_____   *Your name is Claude, right?*

        _____   *Me? No. Dominique.*

_____   *Oh, sorry.*

        _____   *No problem.*

_____   *You're from Paris, right?*

        _____   *Me? No. Brussels.*

_____   *Oh, sorry.*

        _____   *No problem.*

_____   *Well... Bye.*

        _____   *Ciao.*

Exercice de conversation 4.9 Write a conversation between two people who have just met. Person A tries to find out as much as s/he can about Person B (using only the French we've learned so far).

_____

_____

_____

_____

_____

_____

_____

_____

_____

_____

_____

_____

_____

_____

For additional practice, please access [1] youtube.com. Search: "Todd Straus The French Workshop Level 1" and [2] quizlet.com. Search: "TFW Level 1".

Question/Réponse 4

Cover up the **Réponses typiques** below. Then, alternating with a partner, ask and answer the following questions. Glance at the **Réponses typiques** when you need guidance. (Note: There is more than one way to answer some questions correctly.)

Questions

1. Il y a un tableau d'affichage sur des notes?

2. Il y a des tiroirs dans un trombone?

3. Il y a une salle de classe dans une chaise?

4. Il y a un bureau sous des enveloppes?

5. Il y a un sac à dos dans une clé?

6. Il y a une souris dans un clavier?

7. Il y a une table sur une tasse?

8. Il y a un bureau dans un patron?

9. Tu es d'où?

10. Il y a un fauteuil sur un dictionnaire?

11. Lundi est le premier jour de la semaine?

12. Mercredi est le deuxième jour de la semaine?

13. Jeudi est le troisième jour de la semaine?

14. Excusez-moi de vous déranger.

15. Quoi de neuf?

16. Le week-end est mardi et dimanche?

Réponses typiques

1. Non, il y a des notes sur un tableau d'affichage!

2. Non, il y a des trombones dans un tiroir!

3. Non, il y a des chaises dans une salle de classe!

4. Oui, il y a un bureau sous des enveloppes.

5. Non, il y a une clé dans un sac à dos!

6. Non, il y a une souris près d'un clavier!

7. Non, il y a une tasse sur une table!

8. Non, il y a un patron dans un bureau!

9. De Paris. Et toi?

10. Non, il y a un dictionnaire sur un fauteuil!

11. Oui, lundi est le premier jour de la semaine.

12. Non, mardi est le deuxième jour de la semaine.

13. Non, mercredi est le troisième jour de la semaine.

14. Ce n'est pas grave.

15. Rien de special.

16. Non, le week-end est samedi et dimanche.

Nom _____

Histoire/Géographie 4

A. Draw your six-sided map of France with the ten cities, three bodies of water. In addition, show the approximate locations of the Alps and the Pyrenees mountains and seven neighboring countries. (All in French.)

B. Online Search.

① Where does the name "France" come from? Who were the Franks?

_____
_____
_____

② Where does the name "Paris" come from?

_____
_____
_____

Leçon 5

une chambre	un lit	un tapis	une table de nuit
des étagères (f)	une commode	une télévision	une robe de chambre
une lampe	une salle de bains	des lunettes (f)	une affiche
un journal	un oreiller	une couverture	des pantoufles (f)
un poisson	un mobile	des vêtements (m)	un chat
un tableau	un réveil	une fleur	des chaussures (f)

Usage Card no. 12 de (d' before a vowel or an "h") = from, of
à = at, to

Examples: **from** Paris to Brussels = **de** Paris **à** Bruxelles

from the student = **de** l'étudiante   **of** a family = **d'**une famille

to a bedroom = **à** une chambre   **at** the house = **à** la maison

Note these required contractions: **de** + **le** = **du**   **à** + **le** = **au**

de + **les** = **des**   **à** + **les** = **aux**

Study these 5 examples carefully:

1. "the pages of the magazine"
   Incorrect ⟶ les pages **de le** magazine
   Correct ⟶ les pages **du** magazine

2. "to the desk"
   Incorrect ⟶ **à le** bureau
   Correct ⟶ **au** bureau

3. "the color of the curtains"
   Incorrect ⟶ la couleur **de les** rideaux
   Correct ⟶ la couleur **des** rideaux

4. "at the meetings"
   Incorrect ⟶ **à les** réunions
   Correct ⟶ **aux** réunions

5. "near the bed"
   Incorrect ⟶ près **de le** lit
   Correct ⟶ près **du** lit

NOTE: à la, de la, à l' and de l' are all correct.

Examples: All correct ⟶ la couleur **de la** chambre, **à la** porte, **de l'**étudiant, **à l'**écran

Usage Drill

Say whether each of the following is correct or incorrect. Correct those that are wrong.
Alternate with a partner.

1 to the bedroom ⟶ **à la chambre**

2 at the office ⟶ **à le bureau**

3 of the cat ⟶ **de le chat**

4 from the employees ⟶ **de les employés**

5 from a flower ⟶ **de la fleur**

6 from the flower ⟶ **de la fleur**

7 to the cats ⟶ **aux chats**

8 at a boss ⟶ **à un patron**

9 to the cups ⟶ **à les tasses**

10 from the dictionary ⟶ **de le dictionnaire**

11 at the keys ⟶ **à les clés**

12 next to the cat ⟶ **à côté de le chat**

Usage Card no. 13

21 = **vingt et un**   23 = **vingt-trois**   25 = **vingt-cinq**   27 = **vingt-sept**   29 = **vingt-neuf**

22 = **vingt-deux**   24 = **vingt-quatre**   26 = **vingt-six**   28 = **vingt-huit**

Usage Drill

Say the following numbers alternating with a partner.

20, 21, 22, 23, 24, 25, 26, 27, 28, 29, 28, 27, 26, 25, 24, 23, 22, 21, 20, 19, 18, 22, 26, 29, 12, 14
17, 16, 15, 14, 13, 12, 11, 10, 9, 8, 7, 6, 5, 4, 3, 2, 1, 20, 25, 27, 29, 21, 22, 26, 11, 13, 16, 19, 4

a/the	the/a	this/some	some/the
this/a	on these/under some	behind some/in these	a/the
a/far from a	on the/from the	from the/to the	from a/above a
in the/to the	near a/at a	some/to some	to the/near the
a/these	this/from this	to the/some	to the/from the
on a/under these	near the/above the	on a/under a	to the/in some

Conversation 5

Personne 1:	Personne 2:	
Comment est la chambre?		*What's the bedroom like?*
	C'est petit.	*It's small.*
L'autre chambre est grande.		*The other room is large.*
	Comment est ce lit?	*What's this bed like?*
C'est confortable.		*It's comfortable.*
	L'autre lit est inconfortable.	*The other bed is uncomfortable.*
Comment est la télévision?		*What's the television like?*
	C'est vieux.	*It's old.*
Ma télévision est neuve.		*My television is brand new.*
	Comment est le chat?	*What's the cat like?*
C'est adorable.		*It's adorable.*
	Mon chat est moche!	*My cat is ugly!*

Pratique de la conversation

Repeat each line of the Conversation multiple times after your instructor. Then practice the whole Conversation with a partner. Next, cover the French and try repeating the Conversation twice using the English as your guide.

Guide de la prononciation

1. Pronounce: comm**en**t, ch**am**bre, gr**an**de, d**an**s, p**an**toufles, vêtem**en**ts. How are [en], [am] and [an] pronounced?

2. Pronounce: t**a**, m**a**, ch**a**t, confort**a**ble, ador**a**ble. How is [a] pronounced?

3. Pronounce: c**on**fortable, télévisi**on**, m**on**, t**on**, rép**on**se, patr**on**. How is [on] pronounced?

4. Pronounce: b**on**, v**a**, d**an**s, p**an**toufle, t**a**bleau, dev**an**t, t**a**sse, cray**on**, ch**a**t, p**a**tr**on**, ch**am**bre, l**am**pe, p**a**ge, **ar**gent, questi**on**, écr**an**.

Exercices   Leçon 5

Exercice 5.1   Classification. Placer les mots dans une colonne appropriée.

Things We Wear	Heavy Things	Light Things	Others

une chambre

un calendrier

une robe de
   chambre

un tiroir

une pause café

une heure

un mois

un oreiller

des vêtements

5 heures

des toilettes

un journal

un tableau
   d'affichage

une date

des étagères

une couverture

un chat

un argent

une idée

une salle de bains

une enveloppe

une plante verte

un écran

une pantoufle

un tableau

une semaine

une imprimante

un fauteuil

des lunettes

une réunion

un job

une tasse

un poisson

une fleur

une bouteille

une leçon

une commode

une affiche

un clavier

un cahier

un bureau

un mobile

une chaussure

Exercice 5.2 Threes. Put each word into a natural group of three using French words that you know (based on all lessons studied so far).

Example: un crayon, <u>une feuille de papier et une liste</u>

1. une date, _____
2. un lit, _____
3. un journal, _____
4. un sol, _____
5. une pause café, _____
6. des étagères, _____
7. un chat _____
8. un tiroir, _____
9. un document, _____
10. une clé, _____
11. un placard, _____
12. une vidéo, _____
13. une horloge, _____
14. une place, _____
15. des vêtements, _____
16. un patron, _____
17. un mois, _____
18. une plante verte, _____

Exercice 5.3 List 20 items that you come into physical contact with during a typical day. List them in approximate order from morning to night.

1. _____   5. _____
2. _____   6. _____
3. _____   7. _____
4. _____   8. _____

9 _____ 15 _____

10 _____ 16 _____

11 _____ 17 _____

12 _____ 18 _____

13 _____ 19 _____

14 _____ 20 _____

Exercice 5.4 (p. 69) Complete the chart below. (Remember: à + le = au, à + les = aux, de + le = du, de + les = des)

the	at/to the	of/from the	near the
la télévision	à la télévision	de la télévision	près de la télévision
vêtements	vêtements	vêtements	vêtements
mois	étagères	fauteuil	clavier
toilettes	sol	crayons	porte
écran	examen	carte	ordinateur
horloge	horloges	notes	élèves

Exercice de conversation 5.5 (p. 71) Reconstruct Conversation 5 by writing the following sentences in the correct order.

C'est petit.   Comment est le chat?   C'est vieux

Mon chat est moche!   Ma télévision est neuve.   Comment est ce lit?

C'est confortable.   Comment est la télévision?   L'autre chambre est grande.

L'autre lit est inconfortable.   C'est adorable.

Personne 1: Comment est la chambre?

Personne 2:

Personne 1:

Personne 2:

Personne 1:

Personne 2:

Personne 1:

Personne 2:

Personne 1:

Personne 2:

Personne 1:

Personne 2:

Exercice 5.6 (p. 69) from... to... Imagine someone or something going FROM the first item TO the second. (Remember: **de** becomes **d'** before a vowel, and **le, la** become **l'** before a vowel.)

Example 1: un document → une note   **d'un document à une note**
Example 2: le cahier → l'imprimante   **du cahier à l'imprimante**

1. une plante verte → un calendrier _____

2. la réunion → la pause café _____

3. les toilettes → le bureau _____

4. une étudiante → un étudiant _____

5. une lettre → une feuille de papier _____

6. la table → l'employée _____

7. l'écran → les bouteilles _____

8. le secrétaire → la collègue _____

9. les placards → le mur _____

10. la question → les réponses _____

11. un parapluie → une liste _____

12. une fleur → une affiche _____

13. les lunettes → un réveil _____

14. le cahier → des tiroirs _____

15. une robe de chambre → un lit _____

Fill in the missing words. When you've finished, correct yourself in a different color by turning to p. 71.

Personne 1:   **Personne 2:**

Comment est la chambre?

_____ petit.

L'autre _____ grande.

_____ ce lit?

C'est confortable.

L' _____ .

_____ la télévision?

_____ vieux.

Ma _____ neuve.

_____ le chat?

_____ adorable.

Mon _____ moche!

Exercice 5.8 Make five lists below. Each list will include one item that doesn't fit with the others. In class, you will read your lists aloud to a classmate who will identify the one that doesn't fit in each.

1 _____

_____

2 _____

_____

3 _____

_____

4 _____

_____

5 _____

_____

Write the French conversation by translating the English. When you're finished, correct yourself in a different color by turning to p. 71.

Personne 1:   **Personne 2:**

_____

                    _____

_____

                    _____

_____

                    _____

_____

                    _____

_____

                    _____

_____

                    _____

_____

What's the bedroom like?

It's small.

The other room is large.

What's this bed like?

It's comfortable.

The other bed is uncomfortable.

What's the television like?

It's old.

My television is brand new.

What's the cat like?

It's adorable.

My cat is ugly!

Exercice de composition 5.10 Write a 15-sentence description of an extremely messy bedroom. Make sure you use your prepositions (p. 19).

_____

_____

_____

_____

_____

_____

_____

_____

_____

_____

_____

For additional practice, please access [1] youtube.com. Search: "Todd Straus The French Workshop Level 1" and [2] quizlet.com. Search: "TFW Level 1".

Question/Réponse 5

Cover up the **Réponses typiques** below. Then, alternating with a partner, ask and answer the following questions. Glance at the **Réponses typiques** when you need guidance. (Note: There is more than one way to answer some questions correctly.)

Questions

1 Où y a-t-il des livres? (Where are there books?)

2 Où y a-t-il un réveil?
(Where is there an alarm clock?)

3 Où y a-t-il un journal?

4 Où y a-t-il une couverture?

5 Où y a-t-il une affiche?

6 Où y a-t-il des lampes?

7 Où y a-t-il un tapis?

8 Où y a-t-il des étudiants?

9 Où y a-t-il des vêtements?

10 Où y a-t-il des clés?

11 Où y a-t-il un tiroir?

12 Où y a-t-il un tableau?

13 Il y a une table sur la fenêtre?

14 Il y a des chambres dans la souris?

15 Comment est la télévision?

Réponses typiques

1 Il y a des livres sur des étagères.

2 Il y a un réveil à côté d'un lit.

3 Il y a un journal sur une table.

4 Il y a une couverture sur un lit.

5 Il y a une affiche sur un mur.

6 Il y a des lampes sur des commodes.

7 Il y a un tapis sous le lit.

8 Il y a des étudiants dans la salle de classe.

9 Il y a des vêtements dans un placard.

10 Il y a des clés dans un bureau.

11 Il y a un tiroir dans une commode.

12 Il y a un tableau au-dessus d'un lit.

13 Non, la table est loin de la fenêtre.

14 Non. Il y a des souris dans la chambre!

15 C'est vieux.

Histoire/Géographie 5

A. Paris, the French capital, is divided by **La Seine** river. The northern and southern halves of the city are referred to as "**The Right Bank**" and "**The Left Bank**". Administratively, the city is composed of 20 districts called "**arrondissements**". The 20 arrondissements spiral out from the center of Paris.

B. Online Search.

1 Draw Paris as a large circle.

2 Draw the river and its two islands. Label the two islands (in French).

3 Label The Right Bank and The Left Bank (in French).

4 Write the numbers of the 20 arrondissements in their approximate locations on your map.

5 Place and label (in French) the Eiffel Tower.

Leçon

6

un magazine	une guitare	une radio	un chien
une famille	une poupée	une monnaie	un linge
un matin	un soir	une nuit	un verre d'eau
une vue	des camarades de chambre (m. or f.)	une valise	une tablette
des meubles (m)	des bijoux (m)	un rêve	des jouets (m)
des cartes (f)	un sac	un portefeuille	un parfum

Usage Card no. 14 9 Pronoms

Subject Pronouns

je = I　　　　　　　　　　nous = we
tu = you (singular and informal)　vous = you (pural or formal singular)
il = he　　　　　　　　　ils = they
elle = she　　　　　　　　elles = they
on = we

Usage Drills

A. Give the one or two translations of each English pronoun.

1. I (1)
2. we (2)
3. you (2)
4. I (1)
5. he (1)
6. they (2)
7. we (2)
8. you (2)
9. I (1)
10. she (1)
11. they (2)
12. we (2)

B. Practice the following gestures with a partner for two minutes.

1. Say "je" while pointing at yourself.
2. Say "tu" while pointing at your partner.
3. Say "vous" while pointing with both hands at your partner.
4. Say "on" while pointing at yourself and your partner at the same time.
5. Say "nous" while doing the "on" gesture with open hands.
6. Say "ils" while drawing a circle in the air around a group of classmates.
7. Say "elles" while drawing a circle in the air around a group of female classmates.

Now do the gesture for each of the following. Alternate with your partner.

8. je
9. elle
10. on
11. nous
12. vous
13. tu
14. ils
15. vous
16. nous
17. on
18. il
19. tu
20. elles

Usage Card no. 15 il y a vs. voilà

There are two ways to say "There is" or "There are".

There's a book on the table. = **Il y a** un livre sur la table.

vs.

There's the book! = **Voilà** le livre!

With **il y a,** you are <u>describing</u> where something is. With **voilà,** you are <u>showing</u> where something is.

Il y a une porte près de Marie. (You are <u>describing</u> where the door is.)

Voilà la porte! (You are <u>showing</u> where the door is.)

Usage Drill

Would you use **il y a** or **voilà** in the following sentences if you were speaking French?

1 **There is** a door nearby.

2 **There is** the car.

3 **There are** some paper clips in the drawer.

4 **There is** a dog at my house.

5 He said **there's** a large library.

6 **There's** the library!

7 **There's** butter in the fridge.

8 Do you know if **there are** any plates?

Usage Card no. 16 Where is/are ... ?

Où est ... ? = Where is ... ?

Où sont ... ? = Where are ... ?

Examples:

Où est le livre?

Où sont les livres?

Où est Paris?

Où sont Lyon et Bordeaux?

Usage Drill

Ask where each of the following items is.

1 la chambre

2 les cartes

3 les chats

4 le sac a dos

5 les lumières

6 la liste

7 les choses

8 la souris

Where is the … ?	There are the … !	There is a … on a table.	There is a … behind a wall.
Where is the … ?	There's the … !	There is a … in the suitcase.	There's the … !
There is a … in the night.	Where is the … ?	There's the … !	Where's the … ?
from the …	to the …	Where's the …?	There are some … between the dolls.
in the …	from the …	to the …	in a …
There are the …!	There is a … in the magazine	under the …	near the …

Conversation 6

Personne 1:	Personne 2:	
Comment sont tes vêtements?		*What are your clothes like?*
	Mes vêtements sont moches.	*My clothes are ugly.*
Moi, mes vêtements sont mignons.		*My clothes are cute.*
	Comment sont tes pantoufles?	*What are your slippers like?*
Mes pantoufles sont roses.		*My slippers are pink.*
	Moi, mes pantoufles sont bleues.	*My slippers are blue.*
Comment sont tes meubles?		*What is your furniture like?*
	Mes meubles sont élégants.	*My furniture is fancy.*
Moi, mes meubles sont ordinaires.		*My furniture is ordinary.*
	Comment est ta guitare?	*What's your guitar like?*
Ma guitare est excellente.		*My guitar is excellent.*
	Moi, ma guitare est excellente aussi.	*My guitar is excellent too.*

Pratique de la conversation

Repeat each line of the Conversation multiple times after your instructor. Then practice the whole Conversation with a partner. Next, cover the French and try repeating the Conversation twice using the English as your guide.

Guide de la prononciation

1 Pronounce: pause café, tableau, rideaux, chaussure, au-dessus de. How are [au] and [eau] pronounced?

2 Pronounce: toilettes, moi, tiroir, trois, mois, devoirs, toi, soir, mademoiselle. How is [oi] pronounced?

3 Pronounce: excellente, merci, belles, personne, m'appelle, professeur, conversation, verte, question. How is [e] pronounced when it's followed by two consonants?

4 Pronounce: Antoinette, déteste, Belgique, loi, aussi, bois, oiseau, Paul, trois, conversation, tiroir, au-dessus de, chateau, aussi, question.

Nom _____

Exercices   Leçon 6

Exercice 6.1   Classification. Placer les mots dans une colonne appropriée.

Fun	Useful	Beautiful	Others

un parfum   un oreiller   des étagères   une pantoufle   des lunettes

une robe de   des vêtements   une couverture   des bijoux   un clavier
   chambre   un chien   un rêve   des meubles   un soir

une valise   des cartes   un argent   un lit   un job

un sac   des toilettes   un portefeuille   une tablette   un bureau

un(e) camarade   une commode   un tableau   une nuit   une chaussure
   de chambre   un journal   d'affichage   une monnaie

une vue   un cahier   un linge   une famille

une poupée   un matin   un écran   un fauteuil

Exercice 6.2 Groupe de trois. Composer un groupe naturel de trois choses.

Exemple: une valise, <u>des vêtements et un parfum</u>

1. un lit, _____

2. une nuit, _____

3. un magazine, _____

4. une vue, _____

5. des jouets, _____

6. un poisson, _____

7. un sac à dos, _____

8. un job, _____

9. une imprimante, _____

10. un message, _____

11. un rêve, _____

12. des fauteuils, _____

13. un portefeuille, _____

Exercice 6.3 (pp. 3, 19, 69) Les nombres 1-29. Ecrire (Write) ces problèmes d'arithmétique.

1 + 28 = 29 _____

11 − 4 = 7 _____

21 − 2 = 19 _____

17 + 6 = 23 _____

20 − 8 = 12 _____

3 + 18 = 21 _____

16 + 9 = 25 _____

20 - 5 = 15 _____

27 − 14 = 13 _____

Exercice 6.4 (pp. 3, 19, 35, 69) Compléter ce tableau (chart).

some	des nuits	soirs	claviers
the	réunions	job	imprimante
a/an	liste	porte	agenda
this	crayon	cette clé	examen
these	lampes	tiroirs	tasses
of the	message	de la montre	documents
to the	porte	lit	aux chats
in a	enveloppe	mois	journal
near the	chaussures	tableau	argent
next to a	à côté d'une lumière	mot	table
far from a	tableau	loin d'une note	vidéo

Exercice de conversation 6.5 (p. 88) Reconstruct Conversation 6 by writing the following sentences in the correct order.

Mes meubles sont ordinaires.

Ma guitare est excellente.

Mes vêtements sont moches.

Moi, ma guitare est excellente, aussi.

Mes pantoufles sont roses.

Comment sont tes pantoufles?

Moi, mes vêtements sont mignons.

Comment sont tes meubles?

Mes meubles sont élégants.

Comment est ta guitare?

Mes pantoufles sont bleues.

Personne 1: Comment sont tes vêtements?

Personne 2:

Personne 1:

Personne 2:

Personne 1:

Personne 2:

Personne 1:

Personne 2:

Personne 1:

Personne 2:

Personne 1:

Personne 2:

Exercice 6.6 Make five lists below. Each list will include one item that doesn't fit with the others. In class, you will read your lists to a classmate who will identify the one that doesn't fit.

1 _____

_____

2 _____

_____

3 _____

_____

4 _____

_____

5 _____

_____

Fill in the missing words. When you're finished, correct yourself in a different color by turning to p. 88.

Personne 1:

Personne 2:

Comment _____ tes vêtements?

Mes _____ moches.

Moi, mes _____ sont mignons.

_____ tes pantoufles?

Mes _____ roses.

Moi, mes _____ bleues.

_____ meubles?

Mes _____ élégants.

Moi, mes _____ sont ordinaires.

_____ ta guitare?

_____ excellente.

Moi, _____ excellente aussi.

Exercice 6.8 Where might a person put these items? Use one of these prepositions in each answer: **dans, sur, au-dessus de, sous, entre, à côté de, près de**.

Example 1: un portefeuille   <u>dans un tiroir</u>

Example 2: un chat   <u>sur le lit</u>

1 les clés   _____

2 le tableau   _____

3 le réveil   _____

4 une télévision   _____

5 le lit   _____

6 une plante verte _____

7 l'imprimante _____

8 les enveloppes _____

9 l'argent _____

10 la secrétaire _____

11 une lumière _____

12 des choses _____

13 un dictionnaire _____

14 des mots _____

15 les chaises _____

Exercice de conversation 6.9 Write the French conversation by translating the English. When you've finished, correct yourself in a different color by turning to p. 88.

Personne 1:   **Personne 2:**

_____

      _____   *What are your clothes like?*

      _____   *My clothes are ugly.*

_____   *My clothes are cute.*

      _____   *What are your slippers like?*

_____   *My slippers are pink.*

      _____   *My slippers are blue.*

_____   *What is your furniture like?*

      _____   *My furniture is fancy.*

_____   *My furniture is ordinary.*

      _____   *What is your guitar like?*

_____   *My guitar is excellent.*

      _____   *My guitar is excellent too.*

Exercice de composition 6.10   A ten-sentence paragraph. Describe the home of a Mademoiselle Nette, the "neat freak", who always keeps everything in its proper place. Make sure to use: est (is), sont (are), il y a (there is/are) and all of our prepositions (p. 19). Begin your paragraph with "Chez Mademoiselle Nette...* ("At Miss Neat's house...")

For additional practice, please access [1] youtube.com. Search: "Todd Straus The French Workshop Level 1" and [2] quizlet.com. Search: "TFW Level 1".

Question/Réponse 6

Cover up the **Réponses typiques** below. Then, alternating with a partner, ask and answer the following questions. Glance at the **Réponses typiques** when you need guidance. (Note: There is more than one way to answer some questions correctly.)

Questions

1. Où est la clé?

2. Où sont les pantoufles?

3. Où est la salle de bains?

4. Il y a des fleurs ou des crayons dans le tiroir?

5. Il y a deux ou trois personnes dans la réunion?

6. Il y a une valise dans la calculatrice?

7. Il y a des étagères au-dessus de la commode?

8. Comment est ton lit?

9. Comment est ton chat?

10. Une poupée est un jouet ou un meuble?

11. J'adore le matin. Vous aussi?

12. Je déteste le parfum. Vous aussi?

13. Tu détestes quel jour?

14. Dix-huit moins onze font neuf?

15. Vingt-trois moins deux font vingt?

Réponses typiques

1. La clé est dans la porte.

2. Les pantoufles sont sous le lit.

3. La salle de bain est près de ma chambre.

4. Non, les fleurs sont sur la table.

5. Il y a trois personnes.

6. Non, il y a une calculatrice dans la valise!

7. Oui, il y a des étagères au-dessus de la commode.

8. Mon lit est confortable.

9. Mon chat est moche.

10. Une poupée est un jouet.

11. Moi, j'adore le soir.

12. Moi, j'aime bien le parfum.

13. Je déteste dimanche.

14. Non, dix-huit moins onze font sept.

15. Non, vingt-trois moins deux font vingt et un.

Nom _____

Histoire/Géographie 6

A. Draw Paris as a circle. Add and label the **river,** the northern and southern halves of the city (**The Right and Left Banks**) and **The Eiffel Tower.** (All in French.)

PARIS

B. Online Search.

1. Add and label the **two islands** in the river and **Bastille Square.** (in French.)

2. On which island is **Notre-Dame** cathedral located? _____
   Place it on the map above.

3. Identify the following. Include one important date and a very brief historical sketch.

The Eiffel Tower: _____
_____
_____
_____

The Bastille prison: _____
_____
_____
_____

Notre-Dame cathedral: _____
_____
_____
_____

Leçon

7

je	vous	tu	on
une maison	une pièce	une salle à manger	une cuisine

il	il	nous	vous
un coin	une salle de séjour	un couloir	un escalier

ils	elles	on	je
un jardin	un garage	une terrasse	une cave

vous	elles	tu	je
un rez-de-chaussée	un premier étage	un deuxième étage	un objet

tu	je	vous	nous
une nappe	une cheminée	un miroir	un objet d'art

elle	elles	vous	on
une poubelle	un canapé	un cadre	un vase

Usage Card no. 17 La possession

If a pen (masculine) belongs to **je**, then it's . . . . **mon** stylo
If a flower (feminine) belongs to **je**, then it's . . . . **ma** fleur
If things (plural) belong to **je**, then they are . . . . **mes** choses

If a pen belongs to **tu**, then it's . . . . **ton** stylo
If a flower belongs to **tu**, then it's . . . . **ta** fleur
If things belong to **tu**, then they are . . . . **tes** choses

If a pen belongs to **il** or **elle**, then it's . . . . **son** stylo
If a flower belongs to **il** or **elle**, then it's . . . . **sa** fleur
If things belong to **il** or **elle**, then they are . . . . **ses** choses

If a pen belongs to **on** or **nous**, then it's . . . . **notre** stylo
If a flower belongs to **on** or **nous**, then it's . . . . **notre** fleur
If things belong to **on** or **nous**, then they are . . . . **nos** choses

If a pen belongs to **vous**, then it's . . . . **votre** stylo
If a flower belongs to **vous**, then it's . . . . **votre** fleur
If things belong to **vous**, then they are . . . . **vos** choses

If a pen belongs to **ils** or **elles**, then it's . . . . **leur** stylo
If a flower belongs to **ils** or **elles**, then it's . . . . **leur** fleur
If things belong to **ils** or **elles**, then they are . . . . **leurs** choses

Note: If a feminine singular noun begins with a vowel or an "h" (for example: idée or horloge), then you must use the MASCULINE possessive.

> Examples: mon idée, ton horloge, son étudiante

Usage Drill

Say that each item belongs to the person indicated.

> Example: une fleur / je   ma <u>fleur</u>

1 une chaussure / tu

2 des vêtements / vous

3 des lunettes / ils

4 un examen / on

5 des mobiles / elle

6 un oreiller / elles

7 une table de nuit / vous

8 des feuilles de papier / on

9 une télévision / il

10 un chat / elle

11 une couverture / nous

12 une robe de chambre / je

13 une commode / tu

14 une page / on

15 une affiche / il

16 des tapis / je

17 une lampe / je

18 une pantoufle / ils

Usage Card no. 18 Les nombres 30-39

30 = trente	35 = trente-cinq
31 = trente et un	36 = trente-six
32 = trente-deux	37 = trente-sept
33 = trente-trois	38 = trente-huit
34 = trente-quatre	39 = trente-neuf

Usage Drills

A. Say each number, alternating with a partner.

30, 32, 34, 36, 38, 31, 33, 35, 37, 39, 10, 20, 30, 11, 21, 31, 12, 22, 32, 19, 8, 6, 16, 36, 22, 11, 21
13, 33, 23, 14, 34, 25, 15, 5, 16, 26, 36, 17, 1, 21, 31, 28, 18, 9, 29, 39, 22, 24, 31, 8, 17, 16, 5, 1

B. Say each letter alternating with your partner.

Z, R, M, Q, P, A, N, O, D, T, U, B, C, M, V, X, R, E, I, K, J, H, G, E, S, F, W, Y, S, B, U, T
S, F, G, J, L, K, S, R, Q, M, L, V, R, Z, Y, X, W, V, U, T, K, J, G, E, I, U, A, O, E, N, G, J

C. Say each day of the week in French alternating with your partner.

Mon, Fri, Tue, Thu, Sat, Wed, Sun, Tues, Fri, Thu, Wed, Tue, Mon, Sat, Sun, Thu, Tue,
Sun, Sat, Thu, Tue, Mon, Sat, Thu, Tue, Sun, Sat, Wed, Thu, Mon, Tue, Fri, Wed, Sun

je	tu	il	elles
vous	elle	je	nous
je	il	elle	on
vous	nous	je	ils
tu	je	il	il
vous	on	je	elle

Conversation 7

Personne 1:	Personne 2:	
Où est la nappe, s'il vous plaît?		*Where's the tablecloth, please?*
	Sur la table.	*On the table.*
Où est la table?		*Where's the table?*
	Dans la salle à manger.	*In the diningroom.*
Où est la salle à manger?		*Where's the diningroom?*
	A côté de la cuisine.	*Next to the kitchen.*
Où est la cuisine?		*Where's the kitchen?*
	Sous ma chambre.	*Under my bedroom.*
Où est votre chambre?		*Where's your bedroom?*
	Près de la salle de bains.	*Near the bathroom.*
Où est la salle de bains?		*Where's the bathroom?*
	En face des toilettes.	*Across from the toilet.*
Où sont les toilettes?		*Where's the toilet?*
	Juste devant toi!	*Right in front of you!*

Guide de la prononciation

1 Prononcez: manger, chambre, devant, trente, excellente, pantoufle, étudiant, imprimante, plante, vêtements, dimanche, document, enveloppe, calendrier, la France, argent. (Notice that [an], [am], [en] and [em} are all pronounced the same way.)

2 Prononcez: côté, réponse, café, réveil, télévision, école, étagères, réunion, employé, clé. (Notice how [é] is pronounced.)

3 Prononcez: près, pièce, lumière, élève, collègue, problème. (Notice how [è] is pronounced.)

4 Prononcez: clé, lumière, chambre, français, employé, étage, deuxième, réunion, calendrier, chambre, lampe, idée, réponse, près, côté, France, café, élève, problème.

Nom _____

Exercices   Leçon 7

Placer les mots dans une colonne appropriée. **Employer un, une** ou **des aussi.**

Rooms	Other Places	Household Items & Furniture	Others

chambre	poupée	jardin	canapé	lit
toilettes	vêtements	devoirs	rez-de-chaussée	parapluie
cheminée	maison	coin	écran	couloir
vase	pièce	clavier	bijoux	nappe
salle de séjour	premier étage	miroir	salle à manger	poubelle
valise	terrasse	imprimante	meubles	bouteille
garage	cadre	cave	escalier	feuille de papier
tablette	commode	portefeuille	cuisine	

Exercice 7.2 Groupes de trois. Composer un groupe naturel de trois mots ou expressions.

Exemple: une valise, <u>des vêtements et un parfum</u>

1. une table, _____

2. une maison, _____

3. une poubelle, _____

4. un rez-de-chaussée, _____

5. un canapé, _____

6. une salle à manger, _____

7. un objet d'art, _____

8. une cuisine, _____

9. un matin, _____

10. un jouet, _____

11. un coin, _____

12. une horloge, _____

Exercice 7.3 Whose is it? Each item belongs to the person indicated.

Example: une monnaie / je   <u>C'est ma monnaie.</u>

1. un chien / elle _____

2. un matin / nous _____

3. une radio / on _____

4. une vue / je _____

5. une famille / il _____

6. une poupée / elles _____

7. des meubles / je _____

8. des camarades de chambre / elle _____

9. des valises / nous _____

10. des magazines / tu _____

11 une valise / vous _____

12 des parfums / elle _____

13 une nuit / je _____

14 un linge / tu _____

15 une poubelle / il _____

16 un portefeuille / il _____

17 un couloir / nous _____

18 des miroirs / on _____

19 des toilettes / nous _____

20 un rez-de-chaussée / elle _____

Exercice 7.4 (pp. 3, 19, 69, 104) Name two items you might find in each place mentionned.

Example 1: notre salle de séjour ⟶ notre canapé et nos objets d'art
Example 2: un magazine ⟶ des photos et des pages

1 votre salle à manger _____

2 ton jardin _____

3 le couloir _____

4 leur poubelle _____

5 son garage _____

6 une chambre _____

7 ta valise _____

8 notre portefeuille _____

9 une famille _____

10 mon sac _____

11 votre coin _____

12 un vase _____

Exercice 7.5 (pp. 3, 19, 69, 104) Write out the arithmetic problems. <u>Note these terms</u>: **plus** (+), **moins** (-), **fois** (x), **font** (=).

        Example: 2 + 5 = 7   <u>deux **plus** cinq **font** sept</u>

3 x 12 = 36 _____

4 + 21 = 25 _____

8 x 4 = 32 _____

9 + 17 = 26 _____

10 + 28 = 38 _____

36 – 27 = 9 _____

23 + 16 = 39 _____

Exercice 7.6 Write two things that each item mentioned would typically sit between.

        Example: mon livre   <u>entre mon cahier et mon ordinateur</u>

1. votre calculatrice _____
2. notre chat _____
3. ma souris _____
4. une chaise _____
5. notre professeur _____
6. une pièce _____
7. la nappe _____
8. cette poubelle _____
9. le premier étage _____
10. votre couloir _____
11. son portefeuille _____
12. la pause café _____

13 notre patron

_____

14 l'écran

_____

15 ce cadre

_____

Exercice de conversation 7.7 (p. 106) Reconstruct Conversation 7 by writing the following sentences in the correct order.

Où est la table?	Où est la salle de bains?
Où sont les toilettes?	A côté de la cuisine.
Où est votre chambre?	Dans la salle à manger.
Sur la table.	En face des toilettes.
Près de la salle de bains.	Juste devant toi!
Où est la salle à manger?	Où est la cuisine?
Sous ma chambre.	

Personne 1: Où est la nappe, s'il vous plaît?

Personne 2:

Personne 1:

Personne 2:

Personne 1:

Personne 2:

Personne 1:

Personne 2:

Personne 1:

Personne 2:

Personne 1:

Personne 2:

Personne 1:

Personne 2:

Write five lists. Each list will include one item that doesn't fit with the others. In class, you will read aloud your lists. A classmate will identify which item doesn't fit.

1 _____

_____

2 _____

_____

3 _____

_____

4 _____

_____

5 _____

_____

Write the French conversation by translating the English. When you've finished, correct yourself in a different color by turning to p. 106.

Personne 1:   **Personne 2:**

_____

                    _____   *Where's the tablecloth, please?*

                                                    On the table.

_____   *Where's the table?*

                    _____   *In the dining room.*

                                                    Where's the dining room?

_____   *Next to the kitchen.*

                    _____   *Where's the kitchen?*

                                                    Under my bedroom.

_____   *Where's your bedroom?*

                    _____   *Near the bathroom.*

_____ *Where's the bathroom?*

_____ *Across from the toilet.*

_____ *Where's the toilet?*

_____ *Right in front of you!*

Exercice de composition 7.10 Draw an apartment floor plan with at least five rooms. Fill each room with several items. Label each room and item.

For additional practice, please access [1] youtube.com. Search: "Todd Straus The French Workshop Level 1" and [2] quizlet.com. Search: "TFW Level 1".

Question/Réponse 7

Cover up the **Réponses typiques** below. Then, alternating with a partner, ask and answer the following questions. Glance at the **Réponses typiques** when you need guidance. (Note: There is more than one way to answer some questions correctly.)

Questions

1. Y a-t-il une poubelle derrière votre maison?

2. Y a-t-il une salle à manger au rez-de-chaussée chez vous? (chez vous = at your place)

3. Y a-t-il une salle de bains au premier étage chez vous?

4. Y a-t-il deux chambres chez vous?

5. Où y a-t-il des objets d'art chez vous?

6. Où est votre chambre?

7. Où est votre argent?

8. Où est le couloir chez vous?

9. Y a-t-il des toilettes près de votre chambre?

10. Y a-t-il une terrasse dans votre jardin?

11. Où est votre sac à dos?

12. Y a-t-il treize mois?

13. Y a-t-il huit jours dans une semaine?

14. Trente-neuf moins huit font vingt et un?

15. Dix-neuf plus huit font vingt-cinq?

Réponses typiques

1. Oui, il y a une poubelle derrière ma maison.

2. Oui, il y a une salle à manger chez moi.

3. Oui, il y a une salle de bains au premier étage.

4. Non, il y a trois chambres.

5. Il y a des objets d'art dans la salle de séjour.

6. Ma chambre est au rez-de-chaussée.

7. Mon argent est dans mon portefeuille.

8. Le couloir est entre la salle de séjour et la cuisine.

9. Oui, il y a des toilettes près de ma chambre.

10. Oui, il y a une terrasse dans mon jardin.

11. Mon sac à dos est à côté de ma place.

12. Non, il y a douze mois.

13. Non, il y a sept jours.

14. Non, trente-neuf moins huit font trente et un.

15. Non, dix-neuf plus huit font vingt-sept.

Nom _____

Histoire/Géographie 7

A. Draw Paris as a circle. Add and label (en français) the **river,** the two **halves of the city,** the **two islands,** The **Eiffel Tower,** the **Bastille** and **Notre-Dame.**

PARIS

B. Online Search.

1 What is the **postal code** for The Eiffel Tower? _____ _____

What do the first two digits in a Paris postal code represent? _____

_____

What do the last two digits in a Paris postal code represent? _____

_____

② Add the **Louvre** museum to your map.

What is its postal code? _____

Was the Louvre always an art museum? _____

Explain. _____

_____

_____

What ultra-modern **sculpture** is located in the courtyard of the Louvre?

_____

_____

Who designed the courtyard sculpture? _____

When? _____

③ **Notre-Dame.** What is the postal code for the cathedral? _____

What is its architectural style ? _____

Name and explain two innovations of this style? _____

_____

_____

_____

_____

Leçon

8

je	vous	nous	elle
un appartement	un déjeuner	un dîner	un petit déjeuner

vous	ils	on	tu
une rue	un bol	une électricité	un toit

je	elles	vous	nous
un arbre	une émission	une fête	un panneau solaire

ils	je	tu	vous
un(e) voisin(e)	un repas	un quartier	un anniversaire

il	nous	vous	tu
une voiture	une tasse de café	un jardin	un facteur

vous	on	tu	je
un courrier	une boîte aux lettres	un banc	des parents (m)

Usage Card no. 19 The Verbs être and avoir

être (to be)	
je **suis**	nous **sommes**
tu **es**	vous **êtes**
il **est**	ils **sont**
elle **est**	elles **sont**
on **est**	

avoir (to have)	
j'ai	nous **avons**
tu **as**	vous **avez**
il **a**	ils **ont**
elle **a**	elles **ont**
on **a**	

Usage Drill A

Tell your partner whether each of the following items comes from the verb **être** or **avoir**.

1 je suis
2 vous avez
3 elle est
4 j'ai
5 on est

6 j'ai
7 elles sont
8 nous avons
9 elle a
10 il est

11 nous sommes
12 tu as
13 vous êtes
14 ils ont
15 tu es

Usage Drill B

Translate these phrases in one way or two. Alternate with a partner.

1 I am (1)
2 you are (2)
3 she is (1)
4 I have (1)
5 we are (2)

6 I have (2)
7 they are (2)
8 we have (2)
9 she has (1)
10 he is (1)

11 we are (2)
12 you have (2)
13 I have (1)
14 they have (2)
15 you are (2)

Usage Card no. 20 40–69

40 = quarante	**50** = cinquante	**60** = soixante
41 = quarante et un	**51** = cinquante et un	**61** = soixante et un
42 = quarante-deux	**52** = cinquante-deux	**62** = soixante-deux
etc.	etc.	etc.

Usage Drill

Say these numbers, alternating with a partner.

**1, 11, 21, 31, 41, 51, 61, 12, 22, 32, 42, 52, 62, 13, 24, 35, 46, 57, 68, 54, 47, 33, 28, 16, 3, 65
61, 52, 46, 35, 22, 17, 31, 51, 61, 11, 21, 60, 50, 40, 30, 20, 10, 12, 19, 18, 14, 25, 34, 43, 57, 69**

Usage Card no. 21 Les mois

janvier	avril	juillet	octobre
février	mai	août	novembre
mars	juin	septembre	décembre

Usage Drill A

Alternating with a partner, do the following translation drill with the above list of months visible. Then cover up the list and do the drill again.

January, March, May, July, September, November, February, April, June, August, October, December, March, August, February, May, October, January, July, June, November, April, August, March, July, November, July, May, September, December, June, August, February

Usage Drill B

Alternating with a partner, say the French equivalent of these numbers, letters, days and months. (Say the whole French word for each item.)

May, 26, Sat, Y, Tue, Jun, 31, 48, H, Wed, Aug, Mar, 16, 43, 55, Sun, Jan, Thu, Sep, R, E, I, U, 10, 30, 51, B, V, C, Fri, Jul, 61, 13, F, D, Tue, P, O, U, 33, 44, 55, 66, Sat, Mar, Aug, 41, X, R, Wed, E

NOTE: With months, "in" = en

       in May = en mai

       in August = en août

Usage Drill C

Say (in French) in which month each thing might happen.

1 snow

2 your birthday

3 heat

4 rain

5 Easter

6 your favorite day of the year

7 the start of school

8 your perfect weather

11, 21, 31, Feb vous	41, 51, 61, Apr elle	12, 22, 33, Mar on	13, 34, 45, Jan nous
46, 57, 68, Oct ils	14, 25, 46, Sep je	15, 48, 37, Nov vous	16, 49, 52, Dec elles
17, 61, 44, Aug tu	18, 50, 31, May Shingles on a roof je	22, 63, 51, Jun nous	8, 35, 46, Jul vous
10, 40, 50, Aug elles	24, 41, 38, Mar elle	11, 63, 21, Feb tu	24, 1, NQ, 35 ils
48, EUIOT je	LPSD, 52, Jul tu	13, 33, VEBC vous	47, 16, DRZ on
FQLBWHJ ils	69, 58, 47, 36, Jan elles	NEQPAE elle	7, 17, 27, 47 tu

Conversation 8

Personne 1:	Personne 2:	
Où est votre maison?		*Where's your house ?*
	Dans la Rue Martin.	*On Martin Street.*
Où est la Rue Martin?		*Where is Martin Street?*
	Dans le quartier de la gare.	*In the train station district.*
Quelle gare?		*Which train station ?*
	La Gare St. Etienne.	*The St. Steven station.*
A l'est ou à l'ouest?		*To the east or west?*
	A l'est.	*To the east.*
Au sud ou au nord?		*To the south or north?*
	Au nord.	*To the north.*
C'est un quartier agréable?		*Is that a pleasant neighborhood?*
	Oui, très beau et vieux.	*Yes, very beautiful and old.*
Vous avez de la chance!		*You are lucky !*
	Absolument!	*Absolutely!*

Pratique de la conversation

Repeat the conversation after your instructor. Then practice with a partner. When you're ready, cover the French and try repeating again a couple times.

Guide de la prononciation

1 Prononcez: Mar<u>tin</u>, voi<u>sin</u>, jar<u>din</u>, <u>lin</u>ge, <u>cin</u>q, <u>coin</u>, <u>vin</u>gt, ma<u>tin</u>, <u>quin</u>ze, <u>juin</u>, <u>loin</u>.

2 Prononcez: b<u>anc</u>, par<u>ent</u>, d<u>ans</u>, excell<u>ent</u>, p<u>an</u>toufle, gr<u>and</u>, tr<u>ent</u>e, quar<u>ant</u>e.

3 Prononcez: cray<u>on</u>, mais<u>on</u>, m<u>on</u>, émissi<u>on</u>, <u>on</u>ze, b<u>on</u>jour, t<u>on</u>, ball<u>on</u>, poiss<u>on</u>.

4 Prononcez: arg<u>ent</u>, dev<u>ant</u>, s<u>ont</u>, b<u>anc</u>, voi<u>sin</u>, cray<u>on</u>, jar<u>din</u>, <u>lin</u>ge, Fr<u>an</u>ce, émissi<u>on</u>, d<u>ans</u>, mais<u>on</u>, par<u>ent</u>, m<u>on</u>tagne, <u>quin</u>ze, patr<u>on</u>, vêtem<u>ents</u>, gr<u>an</u>de.

Exercices   Leçon 8

Exercice 8.1 Classification. Placer les mots dans une colonne appropriée. **Employer un, une ou des aussi.**

Furniture & Large Things	Places	People & Small Things	Others

anniversaire   fête   miroir   salle à manger
appartement   pièce   cadre   tasse de café
cheminée   repas   meubles   quartier
fauteuil   toit   émission   premier étage
voisine   salle de bains   portefeuille   lit
déjeuner   commode   valise   banc
arbre   jardin   rez-de-chaussée   couloir
voiture   parents   étagères   panneau solaire
boîte aux lettres   rue   poubelle
petit déjeuner   facteur   bijoux

Exercice 8.2 Composer des groupes naturels de trois choses.

Exemple: une valise, <u>des vêtements et un parfum</u>

1. un déjeuner, _____

2. un banc, _____

3. un facteur, _____

4. un panneau solaire, _____

5. un bol, _____

6. une rue, _____

7. une famille, _____

8. une tasse de café, _____

9. une valise, _____

Exercice 8.3 Compléter ce tableau.

my	**mon** banc	cheminée	vidéo
his	tasse	**son** lit	employés
her	argent	valise	imprimante
our	jardin	canapés	élève
your (tu)	objet	terrasse	enveloppe
your (vous)	vue	parfum	examens
their	sac	commodes	oreillers
this	matin	cahier	électricité
some	chambres	escaliers	arbres
these	poupées	pantoufles	**ces** agendas
a	garage	lampe	télévision
the	réveil	lits	heures

Exercice 8.4 (pp. 69, 103, 121) In the following examples, circle the words that make a correct French sentence.

Example : Je / (Vous) êtes / (avez) (une)/ un   corbeille à papier.

1. Vous / Ils   sont / ont   des / une   voiture.

2. Il / Son   parfum / étagères   est / a   dans / sur   la salle de bains.

3. Mes / Mon   parents   a / ont   un / une   liste   de la / des   choses.

4. Vous / Elle   a / ont   sa / son   argent.

5. Ce / Cette   clé   est / a   à côté   de / du   crayon.

6. Je / Tu   as / a   mon / mes   dictionnaires   et   ma / mes   calculatrice.

7. Où   est / sont   vos / votre   voisins?

8. Tu / Vous   avons / as   un / une   mobile   dans / sous   ton / ta   voiture.

Exercice 8.5 Add two suitable items to each list.

Example: mon apartment, mon premier étage → <u>ma chambre, mon rez-de-chaussée</u>

1. votre table, votre bol → _____

2. ton fauteuil, ta table → _____

3. mon jardin, ma vue → _____

4. leur parfum, leur argent → _____

5. sa nuit, sa semaine → _____

6. une personne, une famille → _____

7. le parfum, la poupée → _____

8. ce magazine, cette feuille de papier → _____

9. cette commode, ces étagères → _____

10. mon travail, mon bureau → _____

11. ta voisine, tes parents → _____

12. des repas, des dîners → _____

(p. 124) Recomposer la Conversation 8.

A l'est.	Au sud ou au nord?	Absolument!
Au nord.	C'est un quartier agréable?	A l'est ou à l'ouest?
Dans le quartier de la gare.	Oui, très beau et vieux.	Vous avez de la chance!
Où est la rue Martin?	La gare St. Etienne.	

Personne 1: Où est votre maison?

Personne 2: Dans la rue Martin.

Personne 1:

Personne 2:

Personne 1: Quelle gare?

Personne 2:

Personne 1:

Personne 2:

Personne 1:

Personne 2:

Personne 1:

Personne 2:

Personne 1:

Personne 2:

Exercice 8.7 Write two places where you might find each item mentioned. Use one of these prepositions in each of your answers: **dans, sur, sous, entre, devant, derrière, à côté de, près de, loin de, au-dessus de, à gauche de** (to the left of), **à droite de** (to the right of), **au milieu de** (in the middle of), **avec**.

Example : mon livre   dans mes étagères, à côté de mon lit

1 un repas   _____

2 la gare   _____

3 votre lettre   _____

4 ce jardin _____

6 leur voiture _____

7 mes parents _____

8 un bol _____

9 ton couloir _____

10 leur banc _____

11 une nappe _____

12 ses étudiants _____

Exercice 8.8 (p. 121) Fill in the blanks with the correct form of the verb **être** or **avoir**.

1 Je_____ dans le jardin.

2 Mes voisins _____ dans la rue.

3 Vous _____ un appartement.

4 J' _____ un escalier.

5 Notre courrier _____ sur la table.

6 Mon anniversaire _____ en mai.

7 Le facteur _____ un chat.

8 Mes parents _____ dans la cuisine.

9 Nous _____ une boîte aux lettres.

10 On _____ dans votre quartier.

11 Tu _____ devant la télévision.

12 Les chaussures _____ sous la commode.

13 Les étudiants _____ des problèmes.

14 Votre famille _____ des fleurs.

15 Il y _____ des fleurs dans le jardin.

16 Je _____ votre voisin.

Exercice de conversation 8.9 Write the French conversation by translating the English. When you've finished, correct yourself in a different color by turning to p. 124.

Personne 1:   **Personne 2:**

_____

_____ *Where's your house?*

_____ *On Martin Street.*

_____ *Where's Martin Street?*

_____ *In the train station neighborhood.*

_____ *Which train station?*

_____ *The St. Steven station.*

_____ *To the east or west?*

_____ *To the east.*

_____ *To the north or south?*

_____ *To the north.*

_____ *Is that a pleasant neighborhood?*

_____ *Yes, very beautiful and old.*

_____ *You're lucky!*

_____ *Absolutely!*

Exercice de composition 8.10   Vrai ou faux? Write ten true statements and three obviously false, illogical or absurd statements about you and your posssssions. Use **avoir, être** or **il y a** in each of your statements. In class, you may read aloud your sentences to a partner who will listen and say "C'est vrai." or "C'est faux." after each sentence that you read.

_____

_____

_____

_____

_____

_____

_____

_____

_____

_____

_____

_____

_____

_____

For additional practice, please access [1] youtube.com. Search: "Todd Straus The French Workshop Level 1" and [2] quizlet.com. Search: "TFW Level 1".

Question/Réponse 8

Cover up the **Réponses typiques** below. Then, alternating with a partner, ask and answer the following questions. Glance at the **Réponses typiques** when you need guidance. (Note: There is more than one way to answer some questions correctly.)

Questions

1. Vous avez des chiens?

2. On est au premier étage?

3. Vous êtes près de moi ou loin de moi?

4. Vous avez un réveil dans votre chambre?

5. Vos parents ont trois voitures?

6. Votre maison est dans un quartier résidentiel?

7. Je suis votre professeur?

8. Vous avez de la chance?

9. Bon courage!

10. Vous avez un camarade de chambre?

11. On est dans une salle de classe?

12. Quels sont les sept jours de la semaine?

13. Votre patron a quinze employés?

14. Je suis sur un banc?

15. Il y a des arbres dans votre jardin?

16. Le dîner est à quatre heures?

17. Le déjeuner est à dix heures?

Réponses typiques

1. J'ai un chien.

2. Non, on est au rez-de-chaussée.

3. Je suis près de vous.

4. Oui, j'ai un réveil à côté de mon lit.

5. Non, mes parents ont une voiture.

6. Oui, ma maison est dans un quartier résidentiel.

7. Non, vous êtes mon camarade de classe.

8. Oui, j'ai de la chance.

9. Merci bien. Vous aussi!

10. Oui, j'ai un camarade de chambre.

11. Oui, on est dans une salle de classe.

12. Les sept jours sont lundi, mardi, mercredi, jeudi, vendredi, samedi et dimanche.

13. Non, il a cinq employés.

14. Non, tu es sur une chaise.

15. Oui, il y a trois arbres.

16. Non, mon dîner est à six heures.

17. Non, le déjeuner est à onze heures.

Histoire/Géographie 8

A. Draw and label (en français) Paris, its river, its two halves, two islands, and four sites. Add informational notes in the margins following the example of the note on **Paris**.

Paris: French capital named after Parisii tribe, the first inhabitants of the area in pre-Christian times.

Gothic Architecture:

July 14:

Gustave Eiffel:

PARIS

B. Online Search.

The French Revolution established the French Republic. Is your country a republic?

_____

1 What is a republic? _____

_____

_____

2 Before the Revolution, French society was divided into three classes. Explain. _____

_____

_____

_____

3 Who were the king and queen of France in 1789?_____

What was their fate during the Revolution? _____

_____

Add and label **Place de la Concorde** on the map with the date of the royal executions there.

4 Add and label **The Arch of Triumph** (en français) on your map. What does it commemorate?

_____

_____

5 Who was **Napoléon I**? When did he rule France?_____

_____

_____

_____

Leçon

9

the	this	the	my
un couteau	une fourchette	une cuillère	un dessert

her	the	some	the
une boisson	un verre à vin	un frigo	du poivre du sel

an	this	a	their
des entrées (f)	un plat principal	de la salade	du fromage

my	some	the	our
de l'eau (f)	une assiette	du café	des fruits (m)

this	your	her	his
de la viande	du thé	de la bière	du beurre

your	her	this	the
des serviettes (f)	des légumes (m)	une recette	une carafe

Usage Card no. 22 the vs. some

Where English has one word "the", French has four: **le, la, l', les**.

Where English has one word "some", French has four: **du, de la, de l', des**.

	masc.	fem.	start w/vowel	plur.
the	le	la	l'	les
some	du	de la	de l'	des

Elle a **de l'argent**.   (some money)

Vous avez **des cartes**.   (some cards)

J'ai **de la lumière**.   (some light)

On a **du poivre**.   (some pepper)

Tu as **du courrier**.   (some mail)

Il a **de l'eau**.   (some water)

Usage Drill
Say that there is <u>some</u> of each item.

1 chiens

2 verres à vin

3 fromage

4 salade

5 parfums

6 valises

7 anniversaires

8 électricité

9 linge

10 carafes

11 eau

12 dessert

Usage Card no. 23 12 ---er Verbs

A. The majority of French verbs follow this pattern.

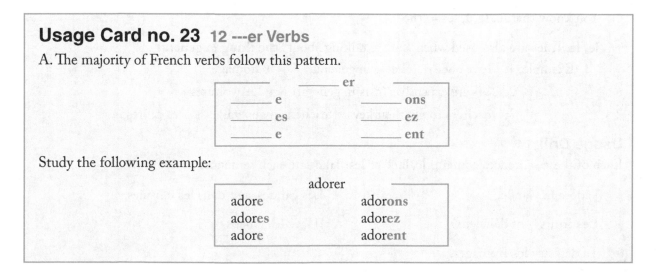

	er
_____ e	_____ ons
_____ es	_____ ez
_____ e	_____ ent

Study the following example:

adorer	
adore	adorons
adores	adorez
adore	adorent

B. Here are 12 extremely common ---er verbs:

adorer	manger	couper	aimer bien
préparer	commencer	détester	terminer
ranger	apprécier	laver	trouver

to love	to eat	to cut	to like
to prepare	to start	to hate	to finish
to put away	to appreciate	to wash	to find

Usage Drill

A. Repeat the above verb forms after your instuctor. Notice that the --e, --es and --ent endings are silent.

B. Pronounce and spell.

1 adorer (vous)   4 préparer (ils)   7 terminer (on)   10 trouver (je)

2 (détester) je   5 manger (nous)   8 couper (elle)   11 ranger (ils)

3 aimer bien (tu)   6 apprécier (elle)   9 laver (nous)   12 commencer (elles)

C. Say (don't write) any one of the verb forms in the chart below. Your partner will say the form immediately to its right.

	je	vous	on	nous	tu	ils
être						
avoir						
adorer						
laver						

Usage Card no. 24 The 2 Meanings of le, la, l', les

1 You know that **le, la, l, les** = "the"

2 **le, la, l', les** are also used when you are talking about "**the thing in general**".
     Example: 1: **I love cheese**. (cheese in general.) —▸ **le** fromage
              2: **Cars** are expensive. (cars in general) —▸ **Les** voitures
              3: **Teachers** forget their keys. (teachers in general) —▸ **Les** professeurs

Usage Drill

Each of these sentences contains **le, la, l'** or **les**. Translate each sentences in two ways.

1 J'adore **la** viande.

2 **Les** fruits sont délicieux.

3 Tu détestes **les** fromages.

4 **Les** carafes sont dans **les** cuisines.

5 Il lave **les** chiens.

ils (adorer)	on (préparer)	vous (apprécier)	ils (couper)
(Jan, Mon, 60)	(Feb, Tue, 53, 40)	(18, Wed, 32, Mar)	(Thu, Apr, 61, 27)
vous (ranger)	tu (manger)	nous (avoir)	elle (laver)
(Fri, May, 44, 64)	(X, D, R, T, E, U)	(Jun, Sat, 16, 51)	(Jul, Sun, R, U)
on (ranger)	vous (aimer bien)	elles (détester)	elle (commencer)
(Aug, Mon, 48, 53)	(Sep, Sun, 20, 30)	(Oct, Jun, Jul, 32)	(B, F, J, G, K, H)
vous (terminer)	je (ranger)	on (avoir)	nous (trouver)
(Oct, Wed, Nov)	(Dec, Feb, Tue)	21, 34, 46, 50	66, 55, 44, 33
vous (avoir)	tu (laver)	nous (préparer)	il (couper)
69, 58, 47, 36	11, 21, 31, 41	29, 37, 25, 13	QWVXPFHGB
on (manger)	nous (terminer)	ils (apprécier)	nous (couper)
KJIEUEUI	Thu, Tue, Aug	10, 17, 16, 1	Wed, Fri, XZW

Conversation 9

Personne 1:	Personne 2:	
Pardon.		*Excuse me.*
	Oui, qu'est-ce que c'est?	*Yes, what is it?*
Y a-t-il un verre à vin dans la cuisine?		*Is there a wine glass in the kitchen?*
	Oui, il y a des verres à vin.	*Yes, there are wine glasses.*
Y a-t-il des tasses aussi?		*Are there cups too?*
	Oui, il y a des tasses dans le placard.	*Yes, there are cups in the closet.*
Quel placard? Le placard à gauche ou à droite?		*Which closet? The closet on the left or right?*
	Le placard à gauche de l'escalier.	*The closet to the left of the stairway.*
Ah, d'accord. Merci beaucoup.		*Oh, OK. Thanks very much.*
	Je vous en prie.	*You're welcome.*
A tout à l'heure.		*See you later.*
	Au revoir. Bon courage.	*Bye. Good luck!*
Merci bien.		*Thanks a lot.*

Pratique de la conversation

Repeat the Conversation after your instructor. Then practice with a partner. When you're ready, cover the French and try repeating again a couple times.

Guide de la prononciation

1. Prononcez: de rien, merci bien, italien, bientôt, chien.

2. Prononcez: des verres, merci, escalier, lecteur mp3, mercredi, la Belgique, plante verte, déteste, toilettes. (Notice how the [e] is pronounced before two consonants.

3. Prononcez: légume, une, voiture, cuisine, nuit, une, vue, couverture, document, bureau.

4. Prononcez: pause café, aussi, fauteuil, boîte aux lettres, au revoir, à gauche, chaussure.

4. Prononcez: chien, bureau, merci, verre, légumes, du, aussi, fauteuil, mur, bientôt.

Exercices   Leçon 9

Exercice 9.1 Classification. Placer les mots dans une colonne appropriée. **Employer un, une du, de la, de l' or des aussi.**

Drinks	Eats	Items for the Table	Meals	Other

fourchette	boisson	eau	bijoux
carafe	beurre	fromage	plat principal
repas	verre à vin	salade	tasse de café
cuillère	toit	émission	sel
légume	fruit	dessert	poivre
déjeuner	couteau	portefeuille	bière
serviette	café	courrier	banc
viande	assiette	rez-de-chaussée	couloir
thé	étagères	entrée	recette
petit déjeuner	facteur	poubelle	

Quatre. Composer un groupe naturel de quatre mots familiers.

Exemple: une valise, <u>des vêtements, un portefeuille, et un parfum</u>

1 un facteur, _____

2 une salade, _____

3 un petit déjeuner, _____

4 un verre, _____

5 une eau, _____

6 une fourchette, _____

7 une entrée, _____

8 un bol, _____

Exercice 9.3 (pp. 19, 35, 103, 138) Complétez ce tableau.

the	his/her	some	this
la fourchette	ses stylos	chaussures	courrier
couteau	eau	du café	nappe
anniversaire	thé	eau	imprimante
quartiers	entrée	tablettes	horloge
nappe	verres	monnaie	ce linge
petit déjeuner	viande	examens	matin
eau	alphabet	argent	nuit
serviettes	chats	mots	examen

Exercice 9.4 (pp. 121, 137) Ecrire la forme indiquée du verbe.

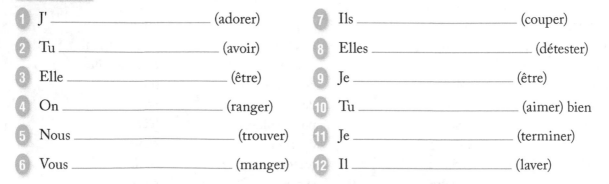

1 J' _____ (adorer)

2 Tu _____ (avoir)

3 Elle _____ (être)

4 On _____ (ranger)

5 Nous _____ (trouver)

6 Vous _____ (manger)

7 Ils _____ (couper)

8 Elles _____ (détester)

9 Je _____ (être)

10 Tu _____ (aimer) bien

11 Je _____ (terminer)

12 Il _____ (laver)

13 Ils _____ (être)   16 Vous _____ (être)

14 Nous _____ (aimer)   17 Nous _____ (détester)

15 Vous _____ (avoir)   18 Tu _____ (être)

Exercice de conversation 9.5 (p. 140) Recomposer la Conversation 9.

Oui, qu'est-ce que c'est?   Quel placard? Le placard à gauche ou à droite?

Merci bien.   Au revoir. Bon courage.

Ah, d'accord. Merci beaucoup.   Oui, il y a des tasses dans le placard.

Y a-t-il des tasses aussi?   Y a-t-il un verre à vin dans la cuisine?

Oui, il y a des verres à vin.   Le placard à gauche de l'escalier.

Je vous en prie.   A tout à l'heure.

Personne 1: Pardon.

Personne 2:

Personne 1:

Personne 2:

Personne 1:

Personne 2:

Personne 1:

Personne 2:

Personne 1:

Personne 2:

Personne 1:

Personne 2:

Personne 1:

Exercice 9.6 In English (and Spanish) there are two ways to formulate a verb: the simple form and the continuous form.

simple	continuous
I eat	I am eating
she washes	she is washing

In French there is only the simple form.

je mange (I eat, I am eating)

elle lave (she washes, she is washing)

Complete this chart.

French Verb Form	=	2 English Verb Forms
1 vous terminez	=	_____ , _____
2 _____	=	I love , _____
3 _____	=	_____ , he is finishing
4 on commence	=	_____ , _____
5 _____	=	they wash , _____
6 nous coupons	=	_____ , _____

Exercice 9.7 Write the two that immediately precede and the two that follow each item given.

Example 1: : quinze ⟶ treize, quatorze / seize, dix-sept

1 mardi ⟶ _____

2 vingt ⟶ _____

3 février ⟶ _____

4 trente-cinq ⟶ _____

5 septembre ⟶ _____

6 avril ⟶ _____

7 un plat principal ⟶ _____

8 le premier étage ⟶ _____

9 quarante ⟶ _____

10 dimanche ⟶ _____

Exercice de conversation 9.8　Write the French conversation by translating the English. When you've finished, correct yourself in a different color by turning to p. 140.

Personne 1:　　　　　　**Personne 2:**

Excuse me.

Yes, what is it?

Is there a wine glass in the kitchen?

Yes, there are wine glasses.

Are there cups too?

Yes, there are cups in the closet.

Which closet? The closet on the left or on the right?

The closet to the left of the stairway.

Oh, OK. Thanks very much.

You're welcome.

See you later.

Bye. Good luck!

Thanks a lot.

Exercice de composition 9.9　Describe a classic diningroom that is all set for a nice dinner. Include the furniture, some decoration, the table setting and some food.

Question/Réponse 9

Cover up the **Réponses typiques** below. Then, alternating with a partner, ask and answer the following questions. Glance at the **Réponses typiques** when you need guidance. (Note: There is more than one way to answer some questions correctly.)

Questions

1. Vous aimez vos grands-parents ou vos enfants?

2. Vous détestez les légumes ou les fruits?

3. Vous aimez le vin français ou italien?

4. Votre famille a une ou deux voitures?

5. Votre mère aime les desserts ou les entrées?

6. Votre salle à manger a des tableaux ou des objets d'art?

7. Quels sont les douze mois de l'année?

8. Vous avez de l'eau dans votre sac à dos aujourd'hui?

9. Récitez l'alphabet, s'il vous plaît.

10. Un fauteuil est un meuble ou un vêtement?

11. Un facteur est une personne ou une chose?

12. Un cahier est une personne ou une chose?

13. Un voisin est une personne ou une chose?

14. Où y a-t-il du courrier?

15. Où y a-t-il de l'eau?

Réponses typiques

1. J'aime mes grands-parents.

2. Non, j'aime les légumes et le fruits.

3. J'aime le vin italien.

4. Ma famille a une voiture.

5. Elle aime les desserts.

6. Ma salle à manger a des tableaux.

7. Les douze mois de l'année sont janvier, février, mars, avril, mai, juin, juillet, août, septembre, octobre, novembre, décembre.

8. Non, mon eau est sur la table.

9. L'alphabet est : A, B, C, D, E, F, G, H, I, J, K, L, M, N, O, P, Q, R, S, T, U, V, W, X, Y, Z.

10. Un fauteuil est un meuble.

11. Un facteur est une personne.

12. Un cahier est une chose.

13. Un voisin est une personne.

14. Il y a du courrier dans une boîte aux lettres.

15. Il y a de l'eau dans une bouteille.

Nom _____

Histoire/Géographie 9

A. Draw and label (en français) **Paris**, its **river**, its two **halves**, two **islands**, **The Eiffel Tower**, **The Bastille**, **The Arch of Triumph**, Notre-Dame, the **Louvre**, **Place de la Concorde**, **Napoléon's tomb**, and the **Franklin Roosevelt subway stop**.

PARIS

B. Online Search.

1　In which arrondissement is Napoléon's tomb located? _____

2　Name the avenue that runs between Place de Concorde and L'Arc de Triomphe.
　　_____. Add this avenue to the map above.

3　What is the Paris subway system called? _____
　　Which American president has a subway stop named after him? _____
　　Add that stop to the map. Why did France honor this American president?
　　_____
　　_____
　　_____

4　Why is the northern half called the "Right" and the southern half called the "Left" Bank
　　rather than the opposite? _____
　　_____
　　_____

Leçon 10

utiliser	acheter	chercher	accepter
je	vous	elle	nous
un plateau	du pain	une bougie	des baguettes (f)

adorer	regarder	trouver	écouter
on	il	vous	elles
des casseroles (f)	une décoration	un glaçon	de la musique

apporter	acheter	utiliser	manger
je	vous	on	tu
de la sauce	une cuisinière	une planche à pain	du sucre

ranger	laver	regarder	aimer bien
elle	on	je	nous
un couvert	une poêle	du rouge	du bleu

utiliser	trouver	apporter	adorer	examiner
vous	elle	on	ils	nous
du jaune	de l'orange	du vert	du violet	du marron

acheter	montrer	recommander	trouver	apprécier
tu	je	vous	elle	ils
du beige	du gris	du rose	du noir	du blanc

Usage Card no. 25 More ---er Verbs

chercher	étudier	montrer	recommander	refuser	regarder
utiliser	garder	apporter	marcher	demander	écouter
acheter	examiner	donner	parler à/de	accepter	oublier

to look for	to study	to show	to recommend	to refuse	to look at, watch
to use	to keep	to bring	to walk	to ask (for)	to listen (to)
to buy	to examine	to give	to speak to/about	to accept	to forget

Usage Drill

A. One partner says the French verb, the other the English. Go through the list multiple times.

B. Now cover up the English and try translating the French. Go through at least twice.

C. Now cover up the French list and translate the English.

D. Fill in the blanks below, then translate in two ways:

Example: (ranger) je _____range_____ → I put away, I'm putting away

1 (laver) vous _____ → _____

2 (apporter) nous _____ → _____

3 (manger) tu _____ → _____

4 (chercher) elle _____ → _____

5 (regarder) on _____ → _____

6 (donner) je _____ → _____

7 (marcher) tu _____ → _____

8 (accepter) il _____ → _____

9 (montrer) ils _____ → _____

10 (terminer) on _____ → _____

11 (oublier) nous _____ → _____

12 (préparer) je _____ → _____

Usage Card no. 26 Which _____?

	sing.	plur.
masc.	Quel bol?	Quels jardins?
fem.	Quelle salade?	Quelles familles?

Usage Drill

Ask "which...?" for each of the following items. Then spell the form of quel.

1 une page

2 un couloir

3 des pages

4 des couloirs

5 du travail

6 des clés

7 des messsagers

8 un objet d'art

Usage Card no. 27 Adjectives

A. In English, adjectives are placed before the noun.

> Examples: a bad dog, your fun party

In French, adjectives are placed after the noun.

> Examples: un café excellent, mon repas délicieux

B. English adjectives have one spelling. French adjectives have four: **masculine** singular and plural and **feminine** singlular and plural.

> Example:

	masc.	fem.
sing	italien	italienne
plur	italiens	italiennes

C. The (masc/fem/sing/plur) form of the noun dictates the form of the adjective. (Never use a masculine adjective to describe a feminine noun, for instance. Or a singular adjective to describe a plural noun.)

> For example:

Incorrect: un livre italienne   Incorrect: des enfants italien

Correct: un livre italien   Correct: des enfants italiens

your	his	our	which?	delicious
délicieux/se	cher/chère	chinois(e)	français(e)	expensive
				Chinese
				French

our	which?	his	her	charming
charmant(e)	élégant(e)	utile	américain(e)	fancy
				useful
				American

the	this	which?	the	excellent
excellent(e)	anglais(e)	blanc/blanche	froid(e)	English
				white
				cold

his	the	some	my	clean
propre	italien/ienne	pure	intense	Italian
				pure
				intense

a	some	which?	this	cute
mignon/onne	intéressant(e)	magnifique	naturel/elle	interesting
				magnificent
				natural

your	his	which?	our	some	ordinary
ordinaire	extraordinaire	mystérieux/se	agréable	épouvantable	extraordinary
					mysterious
					nice
					awful

Conversation 10

Personne 1:	Personne 2:		
Pardon, Hélène.			*Excuse me, Helen.*
	Oui, Robert. Qu'est-ce que c'est?		*Yes, Robert. What is it?*
Y a-t-il des couteaux et des fourchettes dans le tiroir?		*Are there knives and forks in the drawer?*	
	Bien sûr!		*Of course!*
Il y a des cuillères aussi?		*Are there spoons too?*	
	Non, il n'y a pas de cuillères dans le tiroir.		*No, there aren't any spoons in the drawer.*
Où sont les cuillères?		*Where are the spoons?*	
	Sur la table.		*On the table.*
Ah, d'accord.		*Oh, OK.*	
	Y a-t-il des serviettes sur la table aussi?		*Are there napkins on the table too?*
Non, les serviettes sont dans le placard.		*No, the napkins are in the cupboard.*	
	Le placard dans la cuisine?		*The cupboard in the kitchen?*
Oui, c'est ça.		*Yes, that's right.*	
	Merci bien.		*Thanks a lot.*
Je t'en prie.		*You're welcome.*	

Pratique de la conversation

Repeat the Conversation after your instructor. Then practice with a partner. When you're ready, cover the French and try repeating again a couple times.

Guide de la prononciation

1. Prononcez: deux, neuf, déjeuner, deuxième étage, portefeuille, bleu, jeudi, meubles.

2. Prononcez: tableau, rideaux, panneau solaire, bureau, l'eau.

3. Prononcez: rouge, vous, bougie, fourchettes, bonjour, poubelle, couloir, bijoux.

4. Prononcez; tu, rue, sur, salut, étudiant, réunion, mur, calculatrice.

5. Prononcez: deux, tableau, rouge, tu, neuf, rideaux, bougie, panneau, bonjour, réunion, poubelle, bureau, deuxième, couloir, salut.

Exercices   Leçon 10

Exercice 10.1 Classification. Placer les mots dans une colonne appropriée.

Food and Drink	Items in the Kitchen	Pleasing Adjectives	Other

une fourchette   une casserole   anglais   utile
un repas   une poêle   une sauce   intéressant
une cuillère   excellent   une émission   du poivre
cher   un fruit   absolu   un couvert
un déjeuner   un couteau   une cuisinière   du sucre
une serviette   épouvantable   magnifique   charmant
une viande   un verre de vin   une entrée   une planche à pain
des baguettes   froid   agréable   américain
délicieux   propre   chinois   naturel
mignon   bon   intense
un plateau   mystérieux   une assiette
français   élégant   un plat principal

Quatre. Composer un groupe naturel de quatre mots.

Exemple: une valise, <u>des vêtements</u>, <u>un portefeuille</u>, <u>un parfum</u>

1 une eau, _____

2 un buffet, _____

3 des baguettes, _____

4 un violet, _____

5 un sucre, _____

6 une assiette, _____

7 un repas, _____

8 une salle de séjour, _____

9 un cahier, _____

10 une souris, _____

Exercice 10.3 (pp. 19, 35, 137, 154) Complétez ce tableau.

some	which?	this	his
des fleurs	repas?	sac	couverts
poêles	quels examens?	argent	salade
parents	serviettes?	ce bol	escalier
viande	matin?	fenêtre	entrées
jouets	chiens?	objet	sa viande
argent	place?	tasse	étudiante
monnaie	vêtements?	eau	étudiants
lunettes	placard?	nappe	radio

Exercice 10.4 (pp. 121, 138, 153) Fill in each blank with a verb form that makes sense. Be careful to spell the verb correctly. Use at least 12 of the verbs in the following list.

avoir	recommander	aimer bien	demander	étudier
trouver	chercher	examiner	utiliser	garder
accepter	manger	montrer	apporter	oublier
montrer	écouter	laver	ranger	parler à/de

1 Vous _____ un livre.

2 Elle _____ une voiture.

3 Tu _____ du pain.

4 Ils _____ la radio.

5 Je _____ mes clés.

6 Nous _____ des fleurs.

7 Tu _____ tes parents.

8 On _____ un chien.

9 Je _____ un couteau.

10 Ils _____ la carte

11 Vous _____ la chambre.

12 Elles _____ des baguettes.

13 Tu _____ le message.

14 On _____ la cuisine.

15 Vous _____ les jouets.

16 Je _____ mes cousins.

Exercice 10.5 Write out the two that precede and the two that follow each item given.

Example: quinze → <u>treize, quatorze / seize, dix-sept</u>

1 samedi → _____ _____

2 mars → _____

3 août → _____

4 quarante → _____

5 vingt → _____

6 quarante-neuf → _____

7 cinq heures → _____

8 un plat principal → _____

9 trente-deux → _____

10 mercredi → _____

11 douze → _____

12 vingt-sept → _____

13 lundi → _____

Merci bien.

Pardon, Hélène.

Bien sûr!

Où sont les cuillères?

Sur la table.

Oui, c'est ça.

Le placard dans la cuisine?

Ah, d'accord.

Il y a des couteaux et des fourchettes dans le tiroir?

Y a-t-il des serviettes sur la table aussi?

Non, il n'y a pas de cuillères dans le tiroir.

Personne 1:

Personne 2: Oui, Robert. Qu'est-ce que c'est?

Personne 1:

Personne 2:

Personne 1: Il y a des cuillères aussi?

Personne 2:

Personne 1:

Personne 2:

Personne 1:

Personne 2:

Personne 1: Non, les serviettes sont dans le placard.

Personne 2:

Personne 1:

Personne 2:

Personne 1: Je t'en prie.

Exercice 10.7 Create a sentence using all of the given words. Add other words as needed. Change spelling as needed too.

1 vous / accepter / ce / idée / charmant

_____

2 le / jouets / être / propre

_____

3 je / aimer / mon / chaussures / excellent

_____

4 on / ranger / assiette / élégant

_____

5 il y a / fourchettes / tiroir

_____

6 quel / serveurs / recommander / sauce / ?

_____

7 mon / famille / regarder / ce / émission

_____

8 elle / montrer / son / photo / facteur / mignon

_____

Exercice 10.8 (p. 155) Fill in the blank with a logical noun. Before choosing a noun, notice the form (masc, fem, sing, plur) of the adjective.

1	une poupée	mignonne	8	_____ français
2	_____	blanc	9	_____ délicieuse
3	_____	italiens	10	_____ cher
4	_____	élégante	11	_____ américains
5	_____	chinois	12	_____ excellents
6	_____	intéressantes	13	_____ propre
7	_____	utiles		

Write the French conversation by translating the English. When you've finished, correct yourself in a different color by turning to p. 156.

Personne 1:   **Personne 2:**

_____

                    _____

_____

_____

                    _____

_____

                    _____

                    _____

_____

                    _____

_____

                    _____

                    _____

_____

_____

                    _____

_____

                    _____

_____

Excuse me, Helen.

    Yes, Robert, what is it?

Are there knives and forks

in the drawer?

    Of course!

Are there spoons too?

    No, there aren't any spoons

    in the drawer.

Where are the spoons?

    On the table.

Oh, OK.

    Are there napkins on

    the table too?

No, the napkins are in the

cupboard.

    The cupboard in the kitchen?

Yes, that's right.

    Thanks a lot.

You're welcome.

Exercice de composition 10.10   Make a list of 20 things you own and 10 that you would like to own.
Use one of the p. 173 adjectives to describe 10 things on your lists.
(Example: un DVD excellent)

_____

_____

_____

_____

_____

_____

_____

_____

_____

_____

_____

_____

_____

_____

_____

_____

_____

_____

_____

_____

_____

_____

For additional practice, please access [1] youtube.com. Search: "Todd Straus The French Workshop
Level 1" and [2] quizlet.com. Search: "TFW Level 1".

Question/Réponse 10

Cover up the **Réponses typiques** below. Then, alternating with a partner, ask and answer the following questions. Glance at the **Réponses typiques** when you need guidance. (Note: There is more than one way to answer some questions correctly.)

Questions

1. Vous mangez vos légumes?

2. Vous aimez le poivre et le sel sur votre viande?

3. Vous achetez des repas à l'université?

4. Vous utilisez des baguettes ou une fourchette?

5. Vous lavez votre chien?

6. Vous regardez la télévision ou écoutez la radio?

7. Vous montrez des photos à une personne?

8. Vous donnez des documents à votre professeur?

9. Où rangez-vous vos couteaux?

10. Où regardez-vous un DVD?

11. Vous avez des bougies sur votre table de nuit?

12. Vous utilisez une serviette au restaurant?

13. Vous recommandez des émissions?

14. Où avez-vous des décorations?

15. Quelle est la date de votre anniversaire?

Réponses typiques

1. Oui, je mange mes légumes.

2. J'aime le sel.

3. Non, je mange à la maison.

4. J'utilise une fourchette.

5. Oui, je lave mon chien.

6. Je regarde la télévision.

7. Oui, je montre des photos à mes camarades de chambre.

8. Oui, je donne mes devoirs à mes professeurs.

9. Je range mes couteaux dans un tiroir.

10. Je regarde un DVD dans ma salle de séjour.

11. Non, j'ai une tasse et un réveil.

12. Oui, j'utilise une serviette.

13. Oui, je recommande des émissions.

14. J'ai des décorations sur ma porte.

15. C'est le douze août.

Nom _____

Histoire/Géographie 10

A. Place the numbers of the indicated items in their proper location on the map.

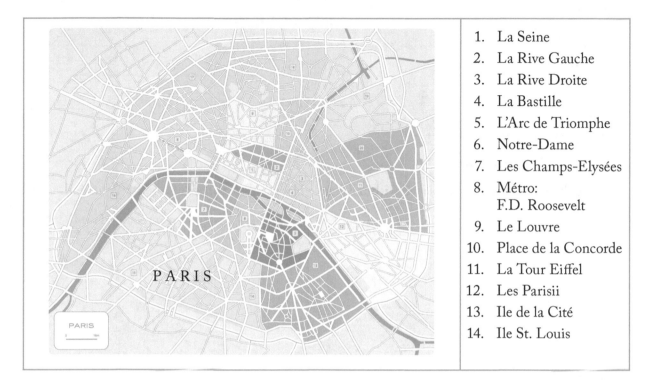

1. La Seine
2. La Rive Gauche
3. La Rive Droite
4. La Bastille
5. L'Arc de Triomphe
6. Notre-Dame
7. Les Champs-Elysées
8. Métro:
   F.D. Roosevelt
9. Le Louvre
10. Place de la Concorde
11. La Tour Eiffel
12. Les Parisii
13. Ile de la Cité
14. Ile St. Louis

B. Online Search.

1 Translate **"The Latin Quarter"** into French. _____ .
Draw and label it on the map above.

2 Why is that neighborhood associated with **Latin**? _____

_____

_____

3 Place and label **La Sorbonne** on the map above. _____

What is La Sorbonne? _____

_____

_____

_____

4 **Le Panthéon** is located just a couple blocks from La Sorbonne. Place and label it on the map.

5 Name four people entombed in Le Panthéon and briefly explain the greatness of each.

A. _____

_____

B. _____

_____

C. _____

_____

D. _____

_____

6 Name the large **park** that is located within a couple blocks of La Sorbonne and Le Panthéon.

_____ Place and label it on the map.

Leçon 11

La famille: 5 générations

un grand-père + une grand-mère

des grands-parents

une mère + un père

un oncle + une tante

des parents

un frère   une soeur   une femme + un mari   un cousin   une cousine

un couple

des cousins

un fils   une fille   une nièce   un neveu

des enfants

un petit-fils   une petite-fille

des petits-enfants

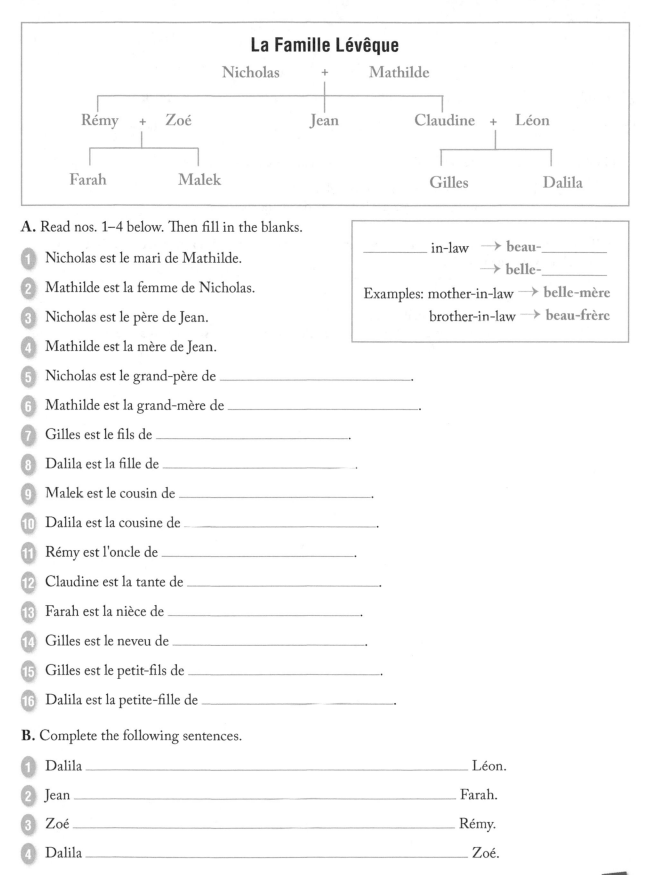

La Famille Lévêque

Nicholas + Mathilde

Rémy + Zoé Jean Claudine + Léon

Farah Malek Gilles Dalila

A. Read nos. 1–4 below. Then fill in the blanks.

| | in-law → beau-_____ |
| → belle-_____ |
| Examples: mother-in-law → **belle-mère** |
| brother-in-law → **beau-frère** |

1 Nicholas est le mari de Mathilde.

2 Mathilde est la femme de Nicholas.

3 Nicholas est le père de Jean.

4 Mathilde est la mère de Jean.

5 Nicholas est le grand-père de _____.

6 Mathilde est la grand-mère de _____.

7 Gilles est le fils de _____.

8 Dalila est la fille de _____.

9 Malek est le cousin de _____.

10 Dalila est la cousine de _____.

11 Rémy est l'oncle de _____.

12 Claudine est la tante de _____.

13 Farah est la nièce de _____.

14 Gilles est le neveu de _____.

15 Gilles est le petit-fils de _____.

16 Dalila est la petite-fille de _____.

B. Complete the following sentences.

1 Dalila _____ Léon.

2 Jean _____ Farah.

3 Zoé _____ Rémy.

4 Dalila _____ Zoé.

5 Léon _____ Claudine.

6 Gilles _____ Léon.

7 Dalila _____ Malek.

7 Malek _____ Nicholas.

C. Confirm each of the statements above by restating each relationship in reverse.

> Example: Nicholas est le mari de Mathilde.
> <u>Oui, Mathilde est la femme de Nicholas.</u>

D. Tell a partner that you are one of the members of the Lévêque family. Your partner will tell you who each of your relatives is.

> Example:
> Moi: Je m'appelle Mathilde.
> Partenaire: Claudine est votre fille. Rémy et Jean sont vos fils ... etc.

Usage Card no. 28 Nombres 60–99

60 = soixante	80 = quatre-vingt
61 = soixante et un	81 = quatre-vingt-un
62 = soixante-deux	82 = quatre-vingt-deux
⋮	⋮
69 = soixante-neuf	89 = quatre-vingt-neuf
70 = soixante-dix	90 = quatre-vingt-dix
71 = soixante et onze	91 = quatre-vingt-onze
72 = soixante-douze	92 = quatre-vingt-douze
73 = soixante-treize	93 = quatre-vingt-treize
74 = soixante-quatorze	94 = quatre-vingt-quatorze
75 = soixante-quinze	95 = quatre-vingt-quinze
76 = soixante-seize	96 = quatre-vingt-seize
77 = soixante-dix-sept	97 = quatre-vingt-dix-sept
78 = soixante-dix-huit	98 = quatre-vingt-dix-huit
79 = soixante-dix-neuf	99 = quatre-vingt-dix-neuf

Usage Drill

A. Say the following numbers alternating with a partner. When you're done, cover up the chart above and try again.

**61, 63, 65, 67, 69, 71, 73, 75, 77, 79, 60, 62, 64, 66, 68, 70, 72, 74, 76, 78, 65, 75, 62, 70, 64
81, 83, 85, 87, 89, 91, 93, 95, 97 ,99, 82, 84, 86, 88, 90, 92, 94, 96, 98, 81, 93, 99, 83, 80, 90**

B. Say the following numbers alternating with your partner.

**1, 11, 13, 20, 21, 22, 30, 31, 33, 40, 41, 44, 50, 51, 55, 60, 61, 66, 70, 71, 77, 55, 37, 62, 75, 25
80, 81, 88, 90, 91, 99, 14, 25, 36, 47, 58, 69, 78, 87, 96, 21, 31, 41, 51, 61, 71, 81, 91, 94, 84, 74
62, 72, 82, 92, 65, 72, 82, 92, 65, 72, 83, 98, 7, 16, 21, 35, 46, 57, 67, 78, 89, 61, 51, 30, 55, 23
69, 70, 81, 94, 61, 74, 85, 91, 88, 77, 66, 55, 44, 33, 22,11, 21, 31, 41, 51, 61, 71, 81. 91, 11, 1**

Usage Card no. 29 The Date

1/1/2000 = **le premier janvier, deux milles**

2/3/2001 = **le deux mars, deux mille un**

5/7/2005 = **le cinq juillet, deux mille cinq**

19/9/1990 = **le dix-neuf septembre, mille neuf cent quatre-vingt-dix**

31/12/1904 = **le trente et un décembre, mille neuf cent quatre**

Usage Drill A

Translate these dates. Alternate with a partner.

1 October 8   3 March 1   5 February 16   7 May 30

2 November 14   4 August 9   6 April 8   8 June 1

Usage Drill B

Translate these dates from numbers to words. Alternate with your partner.
Remember that the first number is the <u>day</u>.

1 3/11/2000   4 21/3/1989   7 8/2/1900   10 20/9/1803

2 1/5/2003   5 15/11/2007   8 18/7/2030   11 16/5/1420

3 12/8/1947   6 1/6/2001   9 10/10/2005   12 14/1/1955

Usage Card no. 30 3 Irregular Verbs

— **être** (to be) —		
je	suis	nous sommes
tu	es	vous êtes
il		
elle	est	ils elles sont
on		

— **avoir** (to have) —		
j'	ai	nous avons
tu	as	vous avez
il		
elle	a	ils elles ont
on		

— **aller** (to go) —		
je	vais	nous allons
tu	vas	vous allez
il		
elle	va	ils elles vont
on		

Usage Drills

A. Pronounce each of the following verb forms. Then say "to be", "to have" or "to go" depending on which verb the form comes from.

Example: **j'ai** → **to have**

1 vous allez   4 on va   7 je suis   10 ils ont   13 on est

2 tu as   5 tu es   8 vous êtes   11 elles sont 14 tu vas

3 elle est   6 nous allons 9 on a   12 je vais   15 j'ai

B. Say the indicated forms. Alternate with your partner..

1 (avoir) vous   3 (aller) tu   5 (avoir) on   7 (avoir) vous   9 (aller) je

2 (être) je   4 (aller) ils   6 (être) on   8 (être) nous   10 (être) elles

C. Cover up the verb chart above and do Drill B again.

Conversation 11

Personne 1:	Personne 2:	
Mon père s'appelle Georges.		*My father's name is Georges.*
	Comment s'appelle votre mère?	*What's your mother's name?*
Elle s'appelle Marianne.		*Her name is Marianne.*
	Moi, mes parents s'appellent Paul et Marthe.	*My parents are named Paul and Martha.*
Vous avez des frères ou des soeurs?		*Do you have brothers or sisters?*
	Une soeur et deux frères. Et vous?	*One sister and two brothers. And you?*
Non, moi, je suis fils/fille unique.		*No, I'm an only child.*
	Quel âge a votre père?	*How old is your father?*
Il est jeune. Ma mère est jeune aussi.		*He's young. My mother is young too.*
	Mes parents sont assez vieux.	*My parents are fairly old.*
Vous êtes marié(e)?		*Are you married?*
	Non, je suis célibataire. Et vous?	*No, I'm single. And you?*
Je suis veuf/veuve.		*I'm widowed.*
	Ah, je suis désolé(e).	*Oh, I'm sorry.*
Merci beaucoup.		*Thank you very much.*

Pratique de la conversation

Repeat the Conversation after your instructor. Then practice it with a partner. When you're ready, cover the French and repeat twice.

Guide de la prononciation

1 Prononcez: désolé, célibataire, marié, février, clé, séjour, téléphone, décembre, réponse.

2 Prononcez: mère, pièce, frère, lumière, derrière, deuxième, chère, cuillère.

3 Prononcez: je, le, ce, quatre, chambre, premier, devant, enveloppe, demander, regarder.

4 Prononcez: mercredi, semaine, employé, écran, collègue, entrée, chère, thé, étagères, pièce, petit déjeuner, téléphone, devant, problème, élève.

Nom _____

Exercices   Leçon 11

Exercice 11.1 Classification. Placer les mots dans une colonne appropriée. Employer un, une, or des aussi.

Males	Females	Both	Things

mère   oncle   tante   cousine
voisin   frère   secrétaire   planche à pain
grand-parent lunettes   soeur   grand-mère
parents   facteur   souris   camarade de chambre
neveu   fille   élève   petite-fille
petit-fils employé   fils   nièce
famille   petit-enfant   patron   voisine
patronne   enfant   couverture   mois

Cinq. Composer un groupe naturel de 5 mots ou expressions.

1 un noir, _____

2 un fils, _____

3 une bougie, _____

4 un grand-père, _____

5 un téléphone, _____

6 un sac à dos, _____

7 une table, _____

8 un appartement, _____

9 une vue, _____

10 des meubles, _____

Exercice 11.3 Compléter ce tableau.

	your (vous)	his	this/these	some	their	which?
frère	votre	son				
sauce						
assiette						
arbre						
voisins						
émissions						
stylo						
parents						

Exercice 11.4 Create a sentence using all of the given words. Add other words or change spelling as needed.

1. je / aller / quartier / près / Tour / Eiffel

   _____

2. pardon / monsieur / où / être / sel / s'il vous plaît / ?

   _____

3. quel / famille / utiliser / voiture / excellent / ?

   _____

4. leur / cousins / chercher / nappe / blanc

   _____

5. je / apporter / bougies / de / mon / soeur

   _____

6. vous / accepter / objet d'art / épouvantable

   _____

7. ils / demander / assiette / vert / et / gris

   _____

8. secrétaire / américain / montrer / documents / intéressant

   _____

Exercice 11.5 Les nombres. Ecrire (Write) ces problèmes d'arithmétique.
(plus = **plus**, minus = **moins**, times = **fois**, equals = **font**)

   Example: 4 x 2 = 8   quatre fois deux font huit

9 x 6 = 54   _____

19 + 42 = 61   _____

4 x 12 = 48   _____

51 - 38 = 13   _____

49 + 28 = 77   _____

11 x 8 = 88 _____

21 + 45 = 66 _____

1 + 69 = 70 _____

98 − 6 = 92 _____

Exercice de conversation 11.6 (p. 175) Recomposer la Conversation 11.

Non, je suis célibataire. Et vous?	Ah, je suis désolé.
Elle s'appelle Marianne.	Moi, mes parents s'appellent Paul et Marthe.
Comment s'appelle votre mère?	Merci bien.
Vous avez des frères et des soeurs?	Je suis veuve.
Il est jeune. Ma mère est jeune aussi.	Quel âge a votre père?
Non, moi je suis fils unique.	Mes parents sont assez vieux.

Personne 1: Mon père s'appelle Georges.

Personne 2:

Personne 1:

Personne 2:

Personne 1:

Personne 2: Une soeur et deux frères. Et vous?

Personne 1:

Personne 2:

Personne 1:

Personne 2:

Personne 1: Vous êtes mariée?

Personne 2:

Personne 1:

Personne 2:

Personne 1:

(p. 170)

Marc + Elise

Aisha + Guillaume   Annette + Thomas

Fatima   Alex   Xavier   Florence   Keisha

1 You are Guillaume. Identify all of your relatives. Include the following words je, mon, ma, notre and s'appelle _____

_____

_____

_____

_____

2 You are Florence. Identify all of your relatives. Include: ma, son, sa, leur, and the verbs être and avoir _____

_____

_____

_____

_____

Exercice 11.8 (p. 174) Write out the following dates.

Example: 5 / 7 / 2012 ⟶ le cinq juillet, deux mille douze

1 / 4 / 1960 ⟶ le premier avril, mille neuf cent soixante

2 / 12 / 2011 _____

14 / 11 / 2005 _____

1 / 3 / 1952 _____

13 / 10 / 2015 _____

7 / 8 / 1820 _____

15 / 6 / 1641 _____

(pp. 137, 174) Compléter ce tableau.

	être	avoir	aller	laver
je				
tu				
on				
nous				
vous				
elles				

Exercice de conversation 11.10 Write the French conversation by translating the English. When you've finished, correct yourself in a different color by turning to p. 175.

Personne 1:   **Personne 2:**

_____

          _____   *My father's name is Georges.*

_____   *What's your mother's name?*

          _____   *Her name is Marianne.*

          _____   *My parents are named Paul and*
          _____   *Martha.*

_____   *Do you have brothers and sisters?*

          _____   *One sister and two brothers.*
          _____   *And you?*

_____   *No, I'm an only child.*

          _____   *How old is your father?*

_____   *He's young. My mother is young too.*

          _____   *My parents are fairly old.*

_____   *Are you married?*

          _____   *No, I'm single. And you?*

_____   *I'm widowed.*

          _____   *Oh, I'm sorry.*

_____   *Thank you very much.*

Exercice de composition 11.11 Write the portrait of a family consisting of three people and a dog. Use **être, avoir, aller, s'appelle, il y a, --er verbs** and **adjectives**.

_____

_____

_____

_____

_____

_____

_____

_____

_____

_____

_____

_____

_____

_____

_____

_____

_____

_____

_____

For additional practice, please access [1] youtube.com. Search: "Todd Straus The French Workshop Level 1" and [2] quizlet.com. Search: "TFW Level 1".

Question/Réponse 11

Cover up the **Réponses typiques** below. Then, alternating with a partner, ask and answer the following questions. Glance at the **Réponses typiques** when you need guidance. (Note: There is more than one way to answer some questions correctly.)

Questions

1. Vous êtes jeune ou vieux/vieille?

2. Vous êtes marié(e) ou célibataire?

3. Les enfants vont à l'école dimanche?

4. Où allez-vous aujourd'hui?

5. Votre grand-mère est la soeur de votre grand-père?

6. Comment s'appelle votre mère?

7. Quelle est la date aujourd'hui?

8. Vingt plus cinquante-deux?

9. Trente plus soixante?

10. Quarante plus cinquante et un?

11. Vous allez à votre boîte aux lettres?

12. Vous avez votre portefeuille?

13. Votre oncle est le fils de votre père?

14. Vous apportez du thé à votre grand-mère?

15. Vos parents vont au supermarché aujourd'hui?

Réponses typiques

1. Je suis jeune.

2. Je suis célibataire.

3. Non, ils vont à l'école de lundi à vendredi.

4. Je vais à la maison de Claude.

5. Non, ma grand-mère est sa femme.

6. Elle s'appelle Marianne.

7. C'est le 30 mai.

8. Soixante-douze.

9. Quatre-vingt-dix.

10. Quatre-vingt-onze.

11. Non, je ne vais pas à ma boîte aux lettres.

12. Oui, j'ai un portefeuille.

13. Non, mon oncle est son frère.

14. Non, je n'apporte pas de thé à ma grand-mère.

15. Non, mes parents ne vont pas au supermarché.

Nom _____

Histoire/Géographie 11

A. Draw **Paris** and label **La Seine, Le Quartier Latin, Place de la Concorde, L'Arc de Triomphe Les Champs-Elysées,** and **Le Jardin du Luxembourg.**

B. Online Search.

PARIS

The government of France includes a **president** and a **prime minister** as well as **two chambers** (similar to the U.S. House of Representatives and the Senate).

1 Place and label the residence of the president on the map. What is the official title of the French president? _____ What is the president's residence called? _____ Who is the current president? _____ How long is a presidential term in office? _____ How many terms can a president serve? _____

2 Place and label the residence of the prime minister on the map. What is the prime minister's residence called? _____ Who is the current prime minister? _____ How are the president's duties different from those of the prime minister? _____
_____
_____
_____

Do the people elect both of them? _____

_____

3 What is the name of the French equivalent of the U.S. House of Representatives? _____

_____. Place and label it

on the map on the preceding page. What is the name of the French equivalent of the U.S. Senate?

_____ Place and label it on the map.

je	tu	il	elle
adorer	être	avoir	chercher
une femme	**un homme**	**un garçon et une fille**	**un homme d'affaires**

nous	un(e) garagiste réparer les voitures	un(e) piéto**n/nne**	un(e) conduc**teur/trice**
recommander		marcher dans la rue	
une femme d'affaires			tourner à droite

on	nous	un auteur	un(e) cuisini**er/ère**
examiner	demander	composer	avoir
un(e) passager/ère****	**un(e) joueu**r/se****	un livre	des légumes

un(e) ouvrier/ère	un(e) serveu**r/se**	on	un(e) client(e)
aimer bien	recommander	consulter	demander
la rue	le dessert	**un(e) polici**er/ère****	une fourchette

vous	il	je	un(e) acteur/actrice
adorer	préférer	admirer	communiquer
un bébé	**un(e) coiffeu**r/se****	**un(e) dentiste**	

un(e) téléspecta**teur/trice**	un(e) scientifique	vous	un vieillard / une vieille dame
aimer bien	examiner	accepter	apporter
une émission	les choses	**un(e) visiteu**r/se****	des fleurs

Usage Card no. 31 4 Verbes irréguliers

être		avoir		aller		venir	
suis	sommes	ai	avons	vais	allons	viens	venons
es	êtes	as	avez	vas	allez	viens	venez
est	sont	a	ont	va	vont	vient	viennent

Usage Drills

A. Pronounce the following verb forms alternating with a partner. The first time through, allow yourself to refer to the chart above. The second time, do the exercise with the verb chart hidden.

1. (être) je
2. (avoir) il
3. (aller) nous
4. (venir) je
5. (être) ils
6. (aller) elle
7. (avoir) tu
8. (venir) elles
9. (avoir) nous
10. (venir) il
11. (aller) tu
12. (avoir) ils
13. (aller) vous
14. (avoir) ils
15. (venir) tu
16. (aller) elles

B. Say (don't write) one of the verb forms that would go into the chart below. Your partner will then say the form immediately to the right of the one that you said.

	je	vous	on	nous	ils	tu
être						
manger						
aller						
ranger						
avoir						
acheter						
venir						

Usage Card no. 32 More ---er Verbs

arriver	admirer	regretter
dîner	communiquer	poser une question
respecter	décider	entrer
copier	avancer	insulter
organiser	préparer	continuer
retourner	réparer	toucher
observer	travailler	développer
consulter	skier	visiter
transporter	distribuer	inviter
préférer	tourner	placer
inventer		

to arrive	to admire	to regret
to eat dinner	to communicate	to ask a question
to respect	to decide	to enter, go in
to copy	to advance, progress	to insult
to organize	to prepare	to continue
to return, go back	to fix, repair	to touch
to observe	to work	to develop
to consult	to ski	to visit
to transport	to distribute	to invite
to prefer	to turn	to place
to invent, make up		

Usage Drill
Create a short sentence with each of the French verbs. Use "je" in each sentence.

Examples: J'arrive à mon appartement.
Je dîne à six heures.

rich happy talkative smart, intelligent	(<u>61</u>, 62, 63) riche	(64, 65, 66) content(e)	(67, 68, 69) bavard(e)	(70, <u>71</u>, 72) intelligent(e)
serious average energetic busy	(73, 74, 75) sérieu<u>x/se</u>	(76, 77, 78) moyen<u>/nne</u>	(79, 78, 77) énergique	(76, 75, 74) occupé(e)
famous experienced hardworking interested	(73, 72, 71) célèbre	(70, 69, 79) expérimenté(e)	(68, 78, 58) travailleu<u>r/se</u>	(65, 75, 45) intéressé(e)
Russian French talented enthusiastic	(80, 81, 82, 83) russe	(84, 85, 86, 87) français(e)	(88, 89, 90, 91) talentueu<u>x/se</u>	(92, 93, 94, 95) enthousiaste
devoted tired in a hurry, rushed (im)patient	(96, 97, 98, 99) dévoué(e)	(<u>61</u>, <u>71</u>, 81, 91) fatigué(e)	(63, 73, 83, 93) pressé(e)	(68, 78, 88, 98) (im)patient(e)
generous fast fun impressed	(99, 98, 96, 95) généreu<u>x/se</u>	(94, 93, 92, 91) rapide	(90, 89, 88, 87) amusant(e)	(86, 85, 84, 83) impressionné(e)

Conversation 12

Personne 1:

Personne 2:

Comment est ton frère?

What's your brother like?

Il est petit, brun, mince
et assez sportif.

*He's small, brown-haired, thin
and fairly athletic.*

Et ta soeur?

And your sister?

Elle est petite, blonde, mince
et très sérieuse.

*She's small, blond, thin
and very serious.*

Moi, ma soeur est grande et énergique.

My sister is tall and energetic.

Quel âge a-t-elle?

How old is she?

Elle a vingt ans. Quel âge ont ton
frère et ta soeur?

*She's twenty. How old are your
brother and sister?*

Mon frère a seize ans, et
ma soeur a dix-huit ans.

*My brother is sixteen, and
my sister is eighteen.*

Vous habitez ensemble?

Do you live together?

Mon frère, non. Mais les autres
membres de la famille, oui.

*My brother, no. But the other
members of the family, yes.*

Dans une maison?

In a house ?

Non, dans un grand appartement.

No, in a big apartment.

Moi, je préfère les appartements.

I prefer apartments.

Guide de la prononciation

1 Prononcez: content, intéressé, français, piéton, enfant, ancien, sont, argent, question, dans, verre à vin, vingt, soixante, maison, parent, marron, orange.

2 Prononcez: professeur, mur, travailleur, heures, chaussure, beurre, soeur, pure, fleur, leur, sur, téléspectateur, voiture.

3 Prononcez: âge, clé, préfère, dévoué, seize, électricité, énergique, employé, riche, côté, personne, poupée, famille, rez-de-chaussée.

4 Prononcez: content, professeur, âge, intéressé, mur, clé, français, piéton, voiture, fleur, personne, sont, argent, chaussure, poupée, Notre-Dame, leur, vêtements, pantoufles, non.

Nom _____

Exercices   Leçon 12

Exercice 12.1   Classification. Ecrire les mots dans une colonne appropriée.

People At Work	Family	Others

un ouvrier

un piéton

une fille

un homme

un dentiste

un vieillard

un garçon

un homme d'affaires

une serveuse

un enfant

un passager

un fils

une conductrice

un joueur

un employé

un client

un garagiste

an auteur

un policier

un petit-fils

une cuisinière

un élève

un facteur

un bébé

une femme

une tante

un téléspectateur

un mari

une coiffeuse

un voisin

une veuve

un scientifique

Exercice 12.2 Associations. Write three things with which each type of person is often associated.

La sorte de personne	3 choses associées
un téléspectateur →	la télévision, son fauteuil, une émission
1 un cuisinier →	_____
2 une scientifique →	_____
3 les enfants →	_____
4 un visiteur →	_____
5 un vieillard →	_____
6 ma mère →	_____
7 un professeur →	_____
8 une femme →	_____
9 mes voisins →	_____
10 un conducteur →	_____

Exercice 12.3 Translate all the words in gray below. Write your translation across the word in gray.

ma fourchette	this **conducteur**	**votre** backyard
some **argent**	**je** show	her **grand-père**
on come	**ils** go	**vous** are
this **oncle**	**elle** listens to **Marc**	you **regardes**
you **avez**	**il** asks for **le bol**	see you later
merci a lot	some **électricité**	which **cuisine?**
your **verres**	**une** clean plate	**les** French objects
which **canapés?**	their **monnaie**	you're welcome
from the **arbre**	to the **poubelles**	near a **gare**

Exercice 12.4 Write what immediately precedes and follows each item given.

Example: quinze ⟶ quatorze et seize

1 mercredi ⟶ _____

2 avril ⟶ _____

3 septembre ⟶ _____

4 quarante-trois ⟶ _____

5 vingt-cinq ⟶ _____

6 soixante-neuf ⟶ _____

7 le premier étage ⟶ _____

8 un homme (think "age") ⟶ _____

9 quatre-vingt-deux ⟶ _____

10 soixante-six ⟶ _____

11 quatre-vingt ⟶ _____

12 quatre-vingt-sept ⟶ _____

13 le déjeuner (think "meals") ⟶ _____

14 samedi ⟶ _____

15 l'université ⟶ _____

Exercice de conversation 12.5 (p. 194) Recomposer la Conversation 12.

Dans une maison?

Elle a vingt ans. Quel âge ont ton frère et ta soeur?

Mon frère, non. Mais les autres membres de la famille, oui.

Et ta soeur?

Elle est petite, blonde, mince et très sérieuse.

Non, dans un grand appartement.

Vous habitez ensemble?

Moi, je préfère les appartements.

Moi, ma soeur est grande et énergique.

Quel âge a-t-elle?

Il est petit, brun, mince et assez sportif.

Personne 1: Comment est ton frère?

Personne 2:

Personne 1:

Personne 2:

Personne 1:

Personne 2:

Personne 1:

Personne 2: Mon frère a seize ans, et ma soeur a dix-huit ans.

Personne 1:

Personne 2:

Personne 1:

Personne 2:

Personne 1:

Exercice 12.6 (pp. 155, 193) Pair each noun with an adjective to create a common description. Remember that adjectives must have the same gender (masc/fem) and number (sing/plur) as the noun that they are paired with.

Nouns

une femme **française**

1. des hommes _____ célèbres _____

2. un enfant _____

3. une rue _____

4. une étudiante _____

5. des repas _____

6. une salade _____

7. un conducteur _____

Adjectives

délicieu<u>x/se</u>
rapide
célibataire
amusant(e)
cher/chère
impressionné(e)
chinois(e)
(im)patient(e)
charmant(e)
pressé(e)
élégant(e)
fatigué(e)
utile
excellent(e)
américain(e)
enthousiaste

8	une passagère _____	anglais(e)
		talentueu<u>x</u>/<u>se</u>
9	un joueur _____	blanc/blanche
		français(e)
10	un auteur _____	froid(e)
		russe
11	une terrasse _____	propre
		intéressé(e)
12	une ouvrière _____	italien/nne
		travailleu<u>r</u>/<u>se</u>
13	des serveurs _____	pure
		expérimenté(e)
14	un policier _____	intense
		célèbre
15	une musique _____	migno<u>n</u>/<u>nne</u>
		intelligent(e)
16	un client _____	magnifique
		énergique
17	des poêles _____	naturel/lle
		sérieu<u>x</u>/<u>se</u>
18	une actrice _____	ordinaire
		content(e)
19	des émissions _____	extraordinaire
		brillant(c)
20	un scientifique _____	agréable
		bavard(e)
21	une radio _____	épouvantable
		sympa
22	des vieillards _____	intéressant(e)
		dévoué(e)
23	un matin _____	mystérieu<u>x</u>/<u>se</u>
		généreu<u>x</u>/<u>se</u>
24	des devoirs _____	marié(e)

Exercice 12.7 Unusual combinations. Pair ten nouns with adjectives that would be exceptional or noteworthy.

Example: un vieillard **mystérieux**!

1 _____

2 _____

③ _____

④ _____

⑤ _____

⑥ _____

⑦ _____

⑧ _____

⑨ _____

⑩ _____

Exercice de conversation 12.8 Write the French conversation by translating the English. When you're finished, correct yourself in a different color by turning to p. 194.

Personne 1:   **Personne 2:**

_____

_____

What's your brother like?

_____

He's small, brown-haired, thin and fairly athletic.

_____

And your sister?

_____

She's small, blond, thin and very serious.

_____

My sister is tall and energetic.

_____

How old is she?

_____

She's twenty. How old are your brother and sister?

_____

My brother is sixteen, and my sister is eighteen.

_____

Do you live together?

_____

My brother, no. But the other members of the family, yes.

_____

In a house?

_____

No, in a large apartment.

_____

I prefer apartments.

First, working with a partner, translate all the verbs in this exercise. Then orally create two sentences for each square.

donner/accepter **1** elle une invitation + généreux/se	laver/utiliser **7** je la voiture + blanc/che	distribuer/transporter **13** ils l'argent + chinois(e)
acheter/manger **2** vous un sandwich + délicieux/se	préférer/préparer **8** nous du café + français(e)	regarder/réparer **14** nous cette horloge + mignon/nne
chercher/trouver **3** on la voiture + magnifique	aimer bien/placer **9** elle le sucre + ordinaire	chercher/trouver **15** vous des gens + bavard(e)
laver/ranger **4** nous des verres + cher/ère	arriver à/aller à **10** je le restaurant + élégant(e)	avoir/poser **16** les gens une question + intéressant(e)
transporter/terminer **5** ils du fruit + extraordinaire	adorer/écouter **11** tu la radio + français(e)	arriver à/venir de **17** je le bureau + propre
retourner à/montrer **6** tu ce quartier + agréable	avoir/parler de **12** vous une vidéo + anglais(e)	garder/utiliser **18** on des choses + utile

First, you will write a ten-sentence portrait of yourself or a friend using a verb from Exercice 12.9 in each sentence. Then you will write a more vivid second draft of the portrait where you will add descriptive adjectives (pp. 155, 193) to each sentence.

For additional practice, please access [1] youtube.com. Search: "Todd Straus The French Workshop Level 1" and [2] quizlet.com. Search: "TFW Level 1".

Question/Réponse 12

Cover up the **Réponses typiques** below. Then, alternating with a partner, ask and answer the following questions. Glance at the **Réponses typiques** when you need guidance. (Note: There is more than one way to answer some questions correctly.)

Questions

1. Quel âge avez-vous?

2. Comment sont les vieillards?

3. Comment sont les bébés?

4. Comment sont les conducteurs?

5. Quelle sorte de magazines aimez-vous?

6. Quelle sorte d'idées avez-vous?

7. Quelle sorte de personnes détestez-vous?

8. Une piétonne est un homme ou une femme?

9. Votre famille habite dans une maison ou dans un appartement?

10. Qu'est-ce que vous achetez? (What do you buy?)

11. Qu'est-ce que vous transportez?

12. Qu'est-ce que vous organisez?

13. Qu'est-ce que vous terminez?

14. Qu'est-ce qu'un serveur apporte?

15. Qu'est-ce qu'un visiteur regarde?

Réponses typiques

1. J'ai vingt-trois ans.

2. Ils sont agréables.

3. Ils sont mignons.

4. Ils sont impatients

5. J'aime les magazines intéressants.

6. J'ai des idées intelligentes.

7. Je déteste les personnes très bavardes.

8. Un piétonne est une femme.

9. On habite dans un appartement.

10. J'achète des fruits.

11. Je transporte mon sac à dos.

12. J'organise des fêtes.

13. Je termine mes devoirs.

14. Un serveur apporte un repas.

15. Un visiteur regarde un monument.

Nom _____

Histoire/Géographie 12

A. Draw **Paris** and label **Notre-Dame, Place de la Concorde, Avenue des Champs-Elysées, L'Arc de Triomphe, Le Palais de l'Elysée** and **L'Hôtel Matignon.** Add 4 brief informational notes in the margins.

**Le Palais de
L'Elysée:**

Le Panthéon:

**L'Hôtel
Matignon:**

**Place de la
Révolution:**

PARIS

B. Online Search.

1 **Victor Hugo.** Where is the author entombed? _____

    Name his 1831 novel. _____

    Name his 1862 novel. _____

2 When did the French Revolution begin and end? _____ _____

    When did Napoléon I's reign begin and end? _____

    What was the condition of the Notre-Dame cathedral when Hugo wrote *Notre-Dame de Paris*?

    _____

    _____

Why? _____

_____

_____

What effect did Hugo's novel have on the fate of the cathedral?

_____

_____

_____

Leçon 13

un(e) styliste	un ingénieur	un(e) ami(e)	un(e) citadin(e)
un barman	un(e) participant(e)	un(e) artiste	un(e) homme/femme de ménage
un(e) réalisateur/trice	un(e) petit(e) ami(e)	des gens	un(e) cycliste
un(e) vendeur/se	un(e) imbécile	un(e) danseur/se	un(e) chanteur/se
un(e) spectateur/trice	un(e) fermier/ière	un(e) athlète	un(e) psychologue
un pompier	un(e) infirmier/ière	"un mec"	"une meuf"

Usage Card no. 33 6 Verbes

être	
suis	sommes
es	êtes
est	sont

avoir	
ai	avons
as	avez
a	ont

aller	
vais	allons
vas	allez
va	vont

venir	
viens	venons
viens	venez
vient	viennent

pouvoir (to be able, can)	
peux	pouvons
peux	pouvez
peut	peuvent

vouloir (to want)	
veux	voulons
veux	voulez
veut	veulent

A. Conjugate and translate each verb form alternating with a partner. The first time through, allow yourself to refer to the chart above. The second time, do the exercise with the chart hidden.

1. (être) vous
2. (avoir) elle
3. (aller) nous
4. (venir) je
5. (pouvoir) tu
6. (vouloir) ils
7. (aller) vous
8. (être) je
9. (vouloir) elle
10. (avoir) je
11. (vouloir) nous
12. (pouvoir) je
13. (aller) je
14. (avoir) elles
15. (être) il
16. (venir) on
17. (pouvoir) vous
18. (venir) vous
19. (pouvoir) ils
20. (vouloir) elles

B. Say (don't write) one of the verb forms that would go into the chart below. Your partner will then say the form immediately to the right of the one that you said.

	je	vous	on	nous	ils	tu
être						
copier						
avoir						
montrer						
aller						
venir						
pouvoir						
toucher						
vouloir						

Usage Card no. 34 Expressions de quantité

1 Use du, de la, de l', des when the quantity is not specific.

> Example: Vous avez des chiens. (You have dogs.)
> Elle veut de l'argent. (She wants money.)

2 To specify quantity, there are numerous expressions all ending in <u>de</u>:

un peu de	une assiette de	une tasse de
beaucoup de	un kilo de	un verre de
un tas de	trop de	une douzaine de
assez de	combien de?	une dizaine de

Exception: quelques = a few

a little	**a plate/bowl of**	**a cup of**
a lot of	**a kilo of**	**a glass of**
lots of	**too much/many**	**a dozen**
enough	**how much/many?**	**about ten**

Examples:

> J'ai beaucoup de papier.
>
> Vous voulez un peu de viande.
>
> Elle achète trop de plantes vertes.
>
> Vous examinez quelques documents.

Usage Drill

Drill: How much/many? Complete each example in two or three ways. Alternate with a partner.

1 Je mange _____ légumes.

2 Vous achetez _____ serviettes.

3 On regarde_____ vidéos.

4 Tu utilises _____ clés.

5 Elle parle à _____ employés.

6 Je trouve _____ trombones.

7 Je place _____ lettres dans la boîte aux lettres.

8 Il y a _____ cartes sur la table.

canadie**n/nne**	bête	amoureu**x/se**	agressi**f/ve**	Canadian stupid in love aggressive
victorieu**x/se**	travailleu**r/se**	divertissant(e)	enthousiaste	winning hardworking entertaining enthusiastic
mexicain(e)	formidable	compréhensi**f/ ve**	adorable	Mexican fantastic understanding adorable
brillant(e)	courageu**x/se**	heureu**x/se**	égoïste	brilliant brave happy, excited selfish
innova**teur/ trice**	compétent(e)	typique	bien habillé(e)	innovative competent typical well dressed
silencieu**x/se**	pauvre	sympa	fort(e)	silent, quiet poor nice, friendly strong

Conversation 13

Au téléphone:	On the phone:
Allô?	*Hello?*
Bonjour, Dominique!	*Hello, Dominique!*
Ah, salut, Claude!	*Oh, hi, Claude.*
Ta soeur est là?	*Is your sister there?*
Non, elle est encore à l'école.	*No, she's still at school.*
Ah bon? Quelle heure est-il?	*Oh really? What time is it?*
Il est deux heures et demie.	*It's two thirty.*
Ah oui! Excuse-moi!	*Oh yes! I'm sorry!*
Pourquoi?	*Why?*
Il est deux heures et demie, pas trois heures et demie! Je suis bête!	*It's two thirty, not three thirty. I'm dumb!*
Ce n'est pas grave.	*No problem.*
L'école finit à trois heures, n'est-ce pas?	*School ends at three, right?*
Oui, ma soeur rentre à trois heures et quart.	*Yes, my sister gets home at three fifteen.*
D'accord. Merci!	*OK. Thanks!*
De rien. A tout à l'heure!	*Sure. See you later!*
Ciao.	*Bye.*

Guide de la prononciation

1 Prononcez: l'école, psychologue, homme, horloge, personne, téléphone, objet, bol, robe, monnaie, votre.

2 Prononcez: trois, moi, miroir, coiffeuse, à droite, voisin, noir, toit, pourquoi, poivre.

3 Prononcez: bon, oncle, conducteur, pardon, sont, bonjour, ton, crayon, montre.

4 Prononcez: octobre, toi, mignon, froid, glaçon, commode, montre, révolution, horloge, miroir.

Nom _____

Exercices   Leçon 13

Exercice 13.1 Classification. Placer les mots dans une colonne appropriée. Employer **un**, **une** ou **des** aussi.

Requires Lots Of Education	Requires Intelligence But Little Education	Requires Physical Coordination	Other

pompier	meuf	imbécile	gens
voisin	psychologue	vendeur	barman
infirmière	athlète	cycliste	citadin
joueur	auteur	scientifique	vieillard
mec	fermier	petit ami	ami
grand-père	spectateur	femme de ménage	ingénieur
danseur	participant	artiste	styliste
ouvrier	chanteuse	patron	

Exercice 13.2 Fill in the following chart by writing the translation across the words in gray.

some	gens		the	écran
too much	argent		my	maison
his	filles	ils give	monnaie
our	enfant		their	appartment
trop de	neighbors	her chaussures cute	
il is eating	du fruit		some	fleurs
about ten	valises		assez de	tea
a commode expensive		some	salade	
enough	argent	je want	bijoux	
lots of	meufs	tu are looking for Marie		

Exercice 13.3 (pp. 155. 193, 211) Pair each adjective with a noun to create a very common description. (Notice the form [masc., fem., sing., plur.] of the adjective when choosing your noun.)

1 _____ chère
2 _____ amusants
3 _____ amoureuse
4 _____ pressée
5 _____ excellent
6 _____ adorable
7 _____ talentueuse
8 _____ travailleur
9 _____ française
10 _____ intéressés
11 _____ intéressante
12 _____ épouvantables

(13) _____ utiles

(14) _____ célibataires

(15) _____ propre

(16) _____ américains

(17) _____ mignonnes

(18) _____ dévoué

(19) _____ forte

(20) _____ silencieuse

Exercice 13.4 (pp. 155, 193, 211) Pair each noun with an adjective to create a very common description.

Example: une femme française

Nouns

(1) un fermier _____

(2) une enfant _____

(3) une meuf _____

(4) des chanteuses _____

(5) une artiste _____

(6) des gens _____

(7) des spectateurs _____

(8) un passager _____

(9) un pompier _____

(10) un barman _____

(11) une participante _____

(12) une ouvrière _____

(13) un petit ami _____

Adjectives

rapide
canadien/nne
amusant(e)
bête
amoureux/se
(im)patient(e)
aggressif/ve
pressé(e)
divertissant(e)
fatigué(e)
travailleur/se
excellent(e)
compréhensif/ve
enthousiaste
adorable
talentueux/se
courageux/se
français(e)
égoïste
russe
innovateur/trice
intéressé(e)
compétent(e)
expérimenté(e)
célèbre
mexicain(e)

(14) une vendeuse _____

(15) un citadin _____

(16) une téléspectatrice _____

(17) des voisines _____

(18) une étudiante _____

(19) un athlète _____

(20) une petite-fille _____

bien habillé(e)
formidable
intelligent(e)
énergique
sérieu<u>x</u>/<u>se</u>
content(e)
brillant(e)
bavard(e)
sympa
dévoué(e)
généreu<u>x</u>/<u>se</u>
cher/chère
pauvre
fort(e)
silencieu<u>x</u>/<u>se</u>

Exercice 13.5 Fill in each blank with the conjugated form of être, avoir, venir, vouloir or pouvoir followed directly by the infinitive of the second verb.

(1) Je _____ **peux venir** _____ (can come)

(2) Vous _____ **voulez manger** _____ (want to eat)

(3) Elle _____ **va trouver** _____ (is going to find)

(4) On _____ (are going to develop)

(5) Ils _____ (come to watch)

(6) Je _____ (can go)

(7) Mon frère _____ (wants to ski)

(8) Tu _____ (can invite)

(9) Nous _____ (are going to ask)

(10) Vous _____ (love to bring)

(11) Elle _____ (can give)

(12) Je _____ (want to buy)

(13) Vous _____ (come to show)

(14) Elles _____ (are going to listen)

(15) Tu _____ (want to fix)

(16) Ils _____ (can clean up)

(17) Elle _____ (is going to wash)

18 On _____ (can eat dinner)

19 Je _____ (want to continue)

20 Le piéton _____ (is going to finish)

Exercice de conversation 13.6 (p. 212) Recomposer la Conversation 13.

Bonjour, Dominique!

Non, elle est encore à l'école.

Ah bon? Quelle heure est-il?

Il est deux heures et demie.

Ah, salut, Claude!

Ce n'est pas grave.

Ah oui! Excuse-moi!

D'accord. Merci!

Ta soeur est là?

Il est deux heures et demie, pas trois heures et demie! Je suis bête!

Ciao.

L'école finit à trois heures, n'est-ce pas?

Oui, ma soeur rentre à trois heures et quart.

Personne 1: Allô?

Personne 2:

Personne 1:

Personne 2:

Personne 1:

Personne 2:

Personne 1:

Personne 2:

Personne 1: Pourquoi?

Personne 2:

Personne 1:

Personne 2:

Personne 1:

Personne 2:

Personne 1: De rien. A tout à l'heure!

Personne 2:

Create a complete sentence using all the given words. When there are two verbs in a row, conjugate the first one and leave the second in the infinitive form. Add words or change spelling as needed.

1 pompier / aller / chercher / chat

_____

2 spectateurs / vouloir / écouter / ce / musique

_____

3 je / aimer / regarder / émission / intéressant

_____

4 quel / femme / pouvoir / trouver / mon / monnaie

_____

5 cousins / vouloir / acheter / un peu / salade

_____

6 vous / détester / utiliser / poêles / italien

_____

7 on / aller / chercher / beaucoup / sucre

_____

8 je / pouvoir / venir / votre / quartier

_____

Exercice de conversation 13.8 Write the French conversation by translating the English. When you're finished, correct yourself in a different color by turning to page 212.

Personne 1:   **Personne 2:**

_____   _Hello?_

_____   _Hello, Dominique!_

_____   _Oh, hi, Claude!_

_____   _Is your sister there?_

_____   _No, she's still at school._

_____   *Oh really? What time is it?*

_____   *It's two thirty.*

_____   *Oh yes! I'm sorry!*

_____   *Why?*

_____   *It's two thirty, not three thirty. I'm dumb!*

_____   *No problem.*

_____   *School ends at three, right?*

_____   *Yes, my sister gets home at three fifteen.*

_____   *OK. Thanks!*

_____   *Sure. See you later!*

_____   *Bye.*

Exercice 13.9   (p. 174) Ecrire ces dates.

Exemples: 5 / 7 / 2012 ⟶ le cinq juillet, deux mille douze

1 / 4 / 1960 ⟶ le premier avril, mille neuf cent soixante

21 / 8 / 2010 _____

25 / 9 / 2005 _____

17 / 4 / 1961 _____

1 / 10 / 2014 _____

2 / 2 / 2222 _____

31 / 12 / 2040 _____

Exercice de composition 13.10 Imagine 10 pictures of different types of people posing. In each picture, imagine the person with two typical things (or people). You will write a total of 15 captions. Use at least one adjective (pp. 155, 193, 211) in each. (Example: Un policier bavard avec des voitures et des citadins.)

_____

_____

_____

_____

_____

_____

_____

_____

_____

_____

For additional practice, please access [1] youtube.com. Search: "Todd Straus The French Workshop Level 1" and [2] quizlet.com. Search: "TFW Level 1".

Question/Réponse 13

Cover up the **Réponses typiques** below. Then, alternating with a partner, ask and answer the following questions. Glance at the **Réponses typiques** when you need guidance. (Note: There is more than one way to answer some questions correctly.)

Questions

1. Vous voulez un peu de dessert?

2. Vous achetez quelques chaussures ou beaucoup de chaussures?

3. Vous écoutez un peu de musique dans votre voiture?

4. Quel âge ont tes parents?

5. Vous mangez un tas de fromage ou un peu de fromage?

6. Vous avez beaucoup de valises ou quelques valises?

7. Qu'est-ce qu'il y a devant un barman?

8. Qu'est-ce qu'il y a devant un étudiant?

9. Qu'est-ce qu'il y a devant des spectateurs?

10. Qu'est-ce qu'il y a devant un enfant?

11. Qu'est-ce qu'il y a devant un petit ami?

12. Qu'est-ce qu'il y a devant un professeur?

13. Qu'est-ce qu'il y a devant un conducteur?

14. Comment est un chanteur?

15. Comment est un imbécile?

16. Comment est un pompier?

17. Comment est une citadine?

18. Comment est un barman?

19. Comment est une cycliste?

20. Comment est un fermier?

Réponses typiques

1. Oui, je veux du dessert. Merci bien.

2. Non, je n'achète pas beaucoup de chaussures.

3. Oui, j'écoute de la musique dans ma voiture.

4. Ma mère a 45 ans et mon père a 47 ans.

5. Je mange un tas de fromage.

6. J'ai trois valises.

7. Il y a des verres devant un barman.

8. Il y a des notes devant un étudiant.

9. Il y a un écran devant des spectateurs.

10. Il y a des jouets devant un enfant.

11. Il y a une personne amoureuse devant un petit ami.

12. Il y a des étudiants devant un professeur.

13. Il y a une rue devant un conducteur.

14. Un chanteur est divertissant.

15. Un imbécile est bête.

16. Un pompier est fort.

17. Une citadine est pressée.

18. Un barman est sympa.

19. Une cycliste est énergique.

20. Un fermier est travailleur.

Histoire/Géographie 13

A. Draw **Paris** with the **river, Napoleon's tomb, La Tour Eiffel, L'Arc de Triomphe, Les Champs-Elysées, Roosevelt's Métro stop** and **Le Quartier Latin.**

PARIS

B. Online Search: The U.S. and France

1 What role did France play in the US. War of Independence?

_____

_____

_____

2 What was "The Louisiana Purchase", and which American and French heads of state signed the deal?

_____

_____

_____

_____

3 How many U.S. states lie within the area of the Louisiana Purchase? _____

4 Translate "World War I" into French. _____

When did WWI start and end? _____

What role did the U.S. play in Europe during World War I? _____

_____

_____

_____

_____

_____

5 Translate "World War II" into French. _____

When did WWII start and end? _____

What role did the U.S. play in Europe during World War II? _____

_____

_____

_____

_____

_____

CONTEST!!!

In the space above, create your entry in the "Best free hand sketch of L'Arc de Triomphe" Contest.

Leçon

14

elle/arriver dans	vous/chercher	on/aller à	tu/entrer dans
une ville	un magasin	un café	une pharmacie
nous/utiliser	je/aller à	elles/venir de	on/visiter
un distributeur de billets	une école	un lycée	une université ("une fac")
je/trouver	vous/travailler à	il/parler de	on/dîner à
une librairie	une pâtisserie	une quincaillerie	un restaurant
tu/aimer bien	on/rester à	vous/danser à	elles/étudier à
un parc	un cinéma	une boîte de nuit	une bibliothèque
nous/recommander	tu/travailler à	on/montrer	je/chercher
un supermarché	une banque	une église	un hôpital
vous/trouver	nous/examiner	elles/dîner sur	je/laver
une rue	un pont	une place	un trottoir

Usage Card no. 35 8 Verbes irréguliers

être		avoir		aller		venir		pouvoir		vouloir	
suis	sommes	ai	avons	vais	allons	viens	venons	peux	pouvons	veux	voulons
es	êtes	as	avez	vas	allez	viens	venez	peux	pouvez	veux	voulez
est	sont	a	ont	va	vont	vient	viennent	peut	peuvent	veut	veulent

devoir (must, to have to)		savoir (know, know how to)	
dois	devons	sais	savons
dois	devez	sais	savez
doit	doivent	sait	savent

Usage Drills

A. Conjugate and translate each verb form alternating with a partner. The first time through, allow yourself to refer to the chart above. The second time, do the exercise with the chart hidden.

1 (être) vous

2 (avoir) elle

3 (aller) tu

4 (venir) nous

5 (pouvoir) ils

6 (devoir) on

7 (être) je

8 (aller) tu

9 (pouvoir) elle

10 (avoir) je

11 (savoir) il

12 (devoir) vous

13 (savoir) je

14 (aller) nous

15 (devoir) je

16 (vouloir) on

17 (venir) je

18 (savoir) nous

19 (devoir) ils

20 (savoir) elles

B. Say one of the verb forms that would go into the chart below. Your partner then says the form immediately below the one that you said.

	je	vous	on	nous	ils	tu
être						
avoir						
aller						
venir						
vouloir						
pouvoir						
devoir						
savoir						

C. Say the English translation of a form in the chart above. Your partner will give the French equivalent.

Usage Card no. 36 Expressions de fréquence

Expressions of frequency go after the verb.

Examples:

Il regarde **toujours** cette émission.	always
Je mange **tout le temps**.	all the time
Il va **souvent** au cinéma.	often
Tu vas **d'habitude**.	usually
Elle accepte **parfois**.	sometimes
Vous écoutez **assez souvent**.	fairly often
Elle regarde **rarement** la télévision.	rarely
Je **n'**écoute **pas** la radio.	not
Je **ne** lave **jamais** ma voiture.	never

Usage Drills

A. Translation.

1. Elle mange parfois
2. Vous avez rarement
3. Ils donnent toujours
4. Je regarde assez souvent
5. Tu n'écoutes pas
6. Elle va d'habitude
7. On veut assez souvent
8. Vous venez toujours
9. Il ne veut jamais
10. J'achète parfois
11. Vous n'avez pas

B. Now disagree with the statements in Usage Drill A.

Example: Elle mange parfois. ⟶ Non, elle mange tout le temps!

C. Translation.

1. You always have
2. She never eats
3. I usually clean up
4. They fairly often find
5. We sometimes give
6. She refuses all the time
7. I rarely listen
8. We often buy
9. You sometimes have
10. He fairly often goes
11. She doesn't come
12. They don't go

Usage Card no. 37 More —er Verbs

penser à	commander	passer	louer
penser que	améliorer	grimper	casser
fermer	rester	répéter	couper
porter	quitter	patienter	chanter

to think about	to order	to pass	to rent
to think that	to improve	to climb	to break
to close	to stay	to repeat	to cut
to carry, to wear	to leave	to wait	to sing

Usage Drills

A. One partner says the French verb, the other the English. Go through the list multiple times.

B. Now cover up the English and try translating from the French. Go through at least twice.

C. Now cover up the French list and translate the English.

je/aller	vous/manger	tu/danser	nous/quitter
never	usually	all the time	not

il/fermer	tu/acheter	je/visiter	ils/patienter
always	rarely	sometimes	often

vous/venir	on/rester	je/retourner	vous/regarder
rarely	sometimes	not	all the time

on/montrer	elle/dîner	nous/adorer	on/chercher
usually	often	always	not

je/acheter	on/améliorer	vous/aller	elles/venir
fairly often	not	never	usually

tu/poser une question	vous/commander	ils/aller	je/travailler
often	always	not	sometimes

Conversation 14

Personne 1:

Où allez-vous aujourd'hui?

Moi, je vais à la bibliothèque.
J'ai besoin de trois livres.

Non, elle va à l'hôpital.

Non, elle travaille à l'hôpital.

Oui, elle est infirmière.

Non, ils vont au cinéma.

Je ne sais pas. Peut-être.

Personne 2:

Je vais à la banque. J'ai besoin
d'argent.

Where are you going today?

I'm going to the bank. I need money.

I'm going to the library.
I need three books.

Maxine va au café?

Maxine's going to the café?

No, she is going to the hospital.

Pourquoi ? Elle est malade?

Why ? Is she sick?

No, she works at the hospital.

Ah bon?

Really?

Yes, she's a nurse.

Jérome et Elise restent à la maison?

Jerome and Elise are staying home?

No, they're going to the movies.

Il y a un bon film ce soir?

Is there a good movie tonight?

I don't know. Maybe.

Guide de la prononciation

1. Prononcez: ils, bibliothèque, kilo, il y a, fatigué, ordinaire, rapide, Paris, aujourd'hui, unique,
avril, cinéma, église, hôpital, ordinateur, pharmacie.

2. Prononcer: intéressant, américain, juin, grimper, quincaillerie, quinze, un, matin, lundi, voisin,
pain, infirmier, salle de bains, à demain.

3. Prononcez: livres, quitter, librairie, lycée, latin, intéressant, ingénieur, citadin, voisin, cuisine,
cousin, cousine, pain, délicieux, jardin, un, lundi, aujourd'hui, à demain.

Exercices   Leçon 14

Exercice 14.1 Classification. Placer les mots dans une colonne appropriée. Employer **un**, **une** ou **des** aussi.

Places Where Visitors Come to Buy	Places Where Visitors Don't Buy

hôpital   rez-de chaussée   maison   cuisine

fac   salle de classe   patisserie   librairie

restaurant   quincaillerie   cinéma   boîte de nuit

bibliothèque   parc   banque   église

distributeur   supermarché   école   lycée

  de billets   magasin   café   pharmacie

ville   quartier   bureau   placard

trottoir   toilettes   pont   jardin

Fill in the following chart by writing the translation across the words in gray.

j' sometimes have	vous always find
une English spectator	des busy city dwellers
ils fairly often know	this farmer **va** to the store
a lot of cyclistes	too many cities have problems
the expensive restaurants	un interesting bridge
there are des trottoirs	how many cinémas?
which bibliothèques?	she can regarder
we must chercher	je know how to **ranger**
vous want to être	ils can show their meubles

Exercice 14.3 Name six things or types of people you would find in each of these places. Avoid repetition as best you can.

1 une ville → _____

_____

2 une fac → _____

_____

3 un supermarché → _____

_____

4 un café → _____

_____

5 un appartement → _____

_____

6 une voiture → _____

_____

7 une cave → _____

_____

8 une assiette → _____

_____

9 une banque → _____

_____

10 une cuisine → _____

_____

11 une tasse → _____

_____

12 une chambre → _____

_____

Exercice de conversation 14.4 (p. 231) Recomposer Conversation 14.

Jérome et Elise restent à la maison?

Ah bon?

Non, elle va à l'hôpital.

Je vais à la banque. J'ai besoin d'argent.

Non, elle travaille à l'hôpital.

Je ne sais pas. Peut-être.

Il y a un bon film ce soir?

Oui, elle est infirmière.

Pourquoi? Elle est malade?

Non, ils vont au cinéma.

Moi, je vais à la bibliothèque. J'ai besoin de trois livres.

Personne 1: Où allez-vous aujourd'hui?

Personne 2:

Personne 1:

Personne 2: Maxine va au café?

Personne 1:

Personne 2:

Personne 1:

Personne 2:

Personne 1:

Personne 2:

Personne 1:

Personne 2:

Personne 1:

Exercice 14.5 Create a complete sentence using all of the given words. Add other words or change spelling as needed. Then translate your sentence into English. (NOTE: When there are two verbs in a row, conjugate the first one and leave the second one in the infinitive form.)

1 on / aller / tout / temps / cinéma

Français: _____

Anglais: _____

2 vous / pouvoir / regarder / ce / garçons / amusant

Français: _____

Anglais: _____

3 elle / aller / savoir / le / réponse

Français: _____

Anglais: _____

4 quel / citadins / ne / venir / pas / fête / ?

Français: _____

Anglais: _____

5 beaucoup / visiteurs / vouloir / avoir / jardins / magnifique

Français: _____

Anglais: _____

6 mon / parents / adorable / apporter / toujours / salade / excellent

Français: _____

Anglais: _____

7 vous / savoir / aller / cinéma / célèbre / quartier

Français: _____

Anglais: _____

Exercice 14.6 Translate these sentences from English to French.

1 We must go to our French library.*

_____

2 This talkative worker has a lot of devoted cousins.

_____

③ These bridges are going to be near your cities.*

_____

④ My grandparents sometimes want to watch horrible TV shows.*

_____

_____

⑤ I don't like to clean up our diningroom.*

_____

*Reminder: When using two verbs in a row, conjugate the first verb. Leave the second in the infinitive form.

Exercice 14.7 Write the French conversation by translating the English. When you've finished, correct yourself in a different color by turning to p. 231.

Personne 1:　　　　　　**Personne 2:**

| | | *Where are you going today?* |

I'm going to the bank. I need money.

I'm going to the library. I need three books.

　　Maxine is going to the café?

No, she's going to the hospital.

　　Why? Is she sick?

No. She works at the hospital.

　　Really?

Yes. She's a nurse.

　　Jérôme and Elise are staying home?

No, they're going to the movies.

　　Is there a good movie tonight?

I don't know. Maybe.

to repeat = __répéter un mot__

to give = _____

to distribute = _____

to love = _____

to arrive = _____

to invite = _____

to bring = _____

to ski = _____

to continue = _____

to prepare = _____

to return = _____

there is/are = _____

to watch = _____

to think = _____

to fix = _____

to improve = _____

to leave = _____

to admire = _____

to wait = _____

to eat = _____

to visit = _____

to develop = _____

to accept = _____

to order = _____

to prefer = _____

to climb = _____

to organize = _____

to stay = _____

to decide = _____

to copy = _____

to ask (for) = _____

to have to = _____

to hate = _____

to go = _____

to insult = _____

to transport = _____

to talk = _____

to like = _____

to look for = _____

to be able = _____

to respect = _____

to listen (to) = _____

to communicate = _____

to come = _____

to carry = _____

to wear = _____

to touch = _____

to work = _____

to buy = _____

to use = _____

to consult = _____

to ask a question = _____

to put away = _____

to invent = _____   to turn = _____

to know = _____   to eat dinner = _____

to show = _____   to finish = _____

to examine = _____   to find = _____

to wash = _____   to know how to = _____

to be = _____   to have = _____

to refuse = _____   to observe = _____

to progress = _____

For additional practice, please access [1] youtube.com. Search: "Todd Straus The French Workshop Level 1" and [2] quizlet.com. Search: "TFW Level 1".

Question/Réponse 14

Cover up the **Réponses typiques** below. Then, alternating with a partner, ask and answer the following questions. Glance at the **Réponses typiques** when you need guidance. (Note: There is more than one way to answer some questions correctly.)

Questions

1. Vous parlez souvent ou rarement?
2. Vous visitez souvent ou rarement un musée?
3. Vous utilisez tout le temps ou jamais le trottoir?
4. On va à l'église quel jour?
5. Vous achetez parfois ou souvent de la viande?
6. Vous skiez souvent ou rarement?
7. Vous travaillez souvent à la bibliothèque?
8. Combien de grands-parents avez-vous?
9. Il y a une quincaillerie dans votre quartier?
10. Où est votre supermarché?
11. Combien de classes avez-vous ce semestre?
12. Vous transportez souvent vos amis?
13. Qu'est-ce que vous réparez?
14. Vous insultez les gens?
15. Où allez-vous rarement?
16. Vous organisez parfois des fêtes?
17. Vous utilisez souvent une planche à pain?
18. Où dînez-vous souvent?

Réponses typiques

1. Je parle souvent.
2. Je visite rarement un musée.
3. J'utilise tout le temps le trottoir.
4. On va à l'église dimanche.
5. J'achète parfois de la viande.
6. Je skie rarement.
7. Oui, je travaille souvent à la bibliothèque.
8. J'ai deux grands-parents.
9. Non, il n'y a pas de quincaillerie dans mon quartier.
10. Mon supermarché est près de mon appartement.
11. J'ai quatre classes.
12. Non, je ne transporte pas souvent mes amis.
13. Je répare ma cuisinière.
14. Non, j'insulte rarement les gens.
15. Je vais rarement au distributeur de billets.
16. Oui, j'organise parfois des fêtes.
17. Oui, j'utilise très souvent ma planche à pain.
18. Je dîne souvent dans ma cuisine.

Nom _____

Histoire/Géographie 14

Online Search

1. How do you say "the French-speaking world" in French? _____

2. French is an official language in how many countries? _____

3. Which of those countries are in Africa? (Write them in French.) _____

_____

4. On the map below, color in the countries that are on the list of countries where French is an official language.

5. On the map, number the three countries where there are the most French speakers.

6. When did the period of French colonialisation of Africa begin? _____

7. When did the last African country gain independence from France? _____

Leçon

15

je/aller	tu/venir	on/rester	nous/visiter
un édifice	un marché	une route	un centre commercial

vous/chercher	elles/admirer	je/arriver	tu/quitter
une autoroute	un gratte-ciel	un monument	une cathédrale

elle/travailler	il/retourner	on/dîner	vous/chercher
une usine	un musée	une gare	une préfecture de police

ils/préférer	on/parler	vous/avoir	ils/trouver
un hôtel	un stade	une piscine	un centre-ville

je/développer	on/aimer bien	je/apprécier	nous/montrer
un quartier résidentiel	une épicerie	un terrain de sport	un théâtre

Usage Card no. 37 Back-to-Back Verbs

When putting two verbs beside one another, conjugate the first one (**Elle va**) and put the second one in the infinitive form (**venir**).

> Examples: Ella **va terminer.** (She's going to finish.)
> Vous **pouvez aller.** (You can go.)

To express what someone **is going to** do, conjugate **aller.**
To express what someone **can** do, conjugate **pouvoir.**
To express what someone **wants to** do, conjugate **vouloir.**
To express what someone **must** do, conjugate **devoir.**
To express what someone **knows how to** do, conjugate **savoir.**
To express what someone **just** did, conjugate **venir + de.**

Usage Drill

A. Translate these back-to-back verbs.

1 je dois aller
2 vous pouvez venir
3 elle vient d'acheter
4 on peut ranger

5 nous allons laver
6 ils savent montrer
7 tu viens de manger
8 elles veulent savoir

7 je vais pouvoir
8 on doit avoir
9 je viens d'utiliser
10 vous devez adorer

B. Translate these back-to-back verbs.

1 I must find
2 you (tu) can watch
3 they are going to eat
4 we just bought

5 she knows how to use
6 I can't come
7 you (vous) are going to be
8 he just came

7 I want ro refuse
8 we just asked
9 I like to give
10 they must have

Usage Card no. 38 Yes/No Questions

To turn a statement into a yes/no question, raise the tone of your voice at the end of the question or start the sentence with est-ce que.

Statements →	Tu as des frères	On vient aujourd'hui.
Questions* →	Tu as des FRÈRES?	On vient aujourd'HUI?
	Est-ce que tu as des frères?	Est-ce qu'on vient aujourd'hui?

*A third way to ask a question (the "inversion form" where the subject and verb switch places) will be practiced in Level 2.

Usage Drill

Turn each of these statements into a question in two ways.

1 Vous êtes intelligente.
2 George veut du lait.

5 Elle a une fleur.
6 Je vais au cinéma

5 On doit venir.
5 Vous achetez des fruits.

je	vous	ils	elle
aller quitter	venir d'arriver à	pouvoir avoir	aller être à

on	nous	elle	on
vouloir travailler à	venir de retourner de	pouvoir dîner à	devoir aller à

vous	je	nous	elles
savoir trouver	aller chercher	vouloir trouver	aller recommander

tu	il	on	vous
vouloir visiter	devoir quitter	aimer être à	venir de parler de

je	ils	on	nous
pouvoir continuer sur	aller aller à	vouloir toucher	devoir admirer

Conversation 15

Personne 1:	Personne 2:	
Il y a un supermarché près d'ici? J'ai besoin de pain.		*Is there a supermarket near here? I need bread.*
	Oui, c'est près du centre commercial.	*Yes, it's near the mall.*
En face de l'hôpital?		*Opposite the hospital?*
	Non, derrière l'hôpital.	*No, behind the hospital.*
Ah oui ! Sur la place!		*Oh yes ! On the square!*
	Oui, c'est ça. Mais c'est fermé aujourd'hui.	*Yes, that's right. But it's closed today.*
Le supermarché est fermé?		*The supermarket is closed?*
	Oui, c'est fermé le dimanche. Mais l'épicerie est ouverte.	*Yes, it's closed on Sundays . But the corner grocery is open.*
Où est-ce?		*Where is that?*
	C'est à trois cents mètres d'ici. Tournez à gauche ici et continuez tout droit.	*It's three blocks from here. Turn left here and keep going straight.*
Merci beaucoup.		*Thanks a lot.*
	De rien. Bonne journée!	*You're welcome. Have a good day!*

Guide de la prononciation

1 Prononcez: bonjour, aujourd'hui, La Tour Eiffel, courageux, amoureux, fourchettes, courrier, journal, toujours, vous, souvent, pouvoir, souris, pantoufles.

2 Prononcez: bureau, sur, voiture, préfecture, chaussure, mur, pure, couverture, journée, du, supermarché.

3 Prononcez: serveur, travailleur, professeur, soeur, fleur, spectateur, beurre, lecteur.

4 Prononcez: couverture, fourchette, courageux, pure, tour, beurre, mur, courrier, chaussure, amoureux, travailleur.

Nom _____

Exercices   Leçon 15

Classification. Write each given word in an appropriate column. Add un or une to each.

Places for Fun/Learning	Places for Buying/Selling	Places for Transport/Safety	Others

hôpital
édifice
terrain de sport
centre commercial
restaurant
hôtel
monument
bibliothèque
pharmacie
café

salle de séjour
route
librairie
parc
quartier résidentiel
usine
supermarché
piscine
école
maison

marché
ville
autoroute
théâtre
musée
banque
stade
lycée
église
cathédrale

magasin
gratte-ciel
boîte de nuit
quincaillerie
gare
distributeur de billets
poste de police
épicerie

Exercice 15.2 List 12 places as well as 2 types of people and 2 things that you would find in each place.

Place	2 People	2 Things

Exercice de conversation 15.3 (p. 249) Reconstruct Conversation 14 by writing the following sentences in the correct order.

Oui, c'est fermé le dimanche. Mais l'épicerie est ouverte.

Où est-ce?

De rien. Bonne journée!

En face de l'hôpital?

Oui, c'est ça. Mais c'est fermé aujourd'hui.

Non, derrière l'hôpital.

Ah oui! Sur la place!

C'est à trois cents mètres d'ici. Tournez à gauche ici et continuez tout droit.

Merci beaucoup.

Oui, c'est près du centre commercial.

Personne 1: Il y a un supermarché près d'ici? J'ai besoin de pain.

Personne 2:

Personne 1:

Personne 2:

Personne 1:

Personne 2:

Personne 1: Le supermarché est fermé?

Personne 2:

Personne 1:

Personne 2:

Personne 1:

Personne 2:

Exercise 15.4 (p. 247) Turn each statement into a question using Est-ce que/qu'.

1. Vous êtes française. → _____

2. Elle va à Paris. → _____

3. Martine mange au restaurant. → _____

4. Nos parents ne savent pas. → _____

Exercise 15.5 Rewrite each sentence making the indicated change. You will make each change to the sentence immediately above it.

1. Vous avez un chat.
(add fun) _____Vous avez un chat amusant._____
(change cat to cats) _____Vous avez des chats amusants._____
(change you to she) _____
(add a lot of) _____
(add is going to) _____
(add sir at the end) _____

2. J'apporte du vin.
(change I to They) _____
(change wine to wines) _____
(add must) _____
(change some to these) _____
(add not) _____
(add expensive) _____

3. Mon voisin vient de France.
(make neighbor plural) _____
(change to Belgium) _____
(make neighbors feminine) _____
(add chatty) _____
(change come to are) _____
(add can) _____
(turn sentence into question) _____

4 Les parents sont toujours heureux.

(change parents to uncle) _____

(change always to often) _____

(change the to their) _____

(add not) _____

(turn sentence into a question) _____

(change uncle to aunt) _____

(add French) _____

Exercice de conversation 15.6 Write the French conversation by translating the English. When you've finished, correct yourself in a different color by turning to p. 249.

Personne 1:   **Personne 2:**

_____   *Is there a supermarket near here?*
_____   *I need bread.*

              _____   *Yes, it's near the mall.*

_____   *Opposite the hospital?*

              _____   *No, behind the hospital.*

_____   *Oh yes! On the square!*

              _____   *Yes, that's right. But it's*
              _____   *closed today.*

_____   *The supermarket is closed?*

              _____   *Yes. It's closed on Sundays.*
              _____   *But the corner grocery is open.*

_____   *Where is that?*

              _____   *It's three blocks from here.*
              _____   *Turn left here and keep going*
              _____   *straight.*

_____   *Thanks a lot.*

              _____   *You're welcome. Have a good day!*

Exercice de composition 15.7   An Interview. Write a French journalist's interview with an average citizen of your country. The journalist will ask a total of 10 questions. Your countryman will answer 8 of them in unsurprising fashion. However, two of the answers will be unusual.

_____

_____

_____

_____

_____

_____

_____

_____

_____

_____

_____

_____

_____

_____

_____

_____

_____

_____

_____

For additional practice, please access [1] youtube.com. Search: "Todd Straus The French Workshop Level 1" and [2] quizlet.com. Search: "TFW Level 1".

Question/Réponse 15

Cover up the **Réponses typiques** below. Then, alternating with a partner, ask and answer the following questions. Glance at the **Réponses typiques** when you need guidance. (Note: There is more than one way to answer some questions correctly.)

Questions

1 Est-ce que la France est loin des Etats-Unis ou loin de l'Italie?

2 Est-ce que l'Espagne est près de la France ou près du Canada?

3 Est-ce que la Belgique est à côté du Luxembourg ou de l'Espagne?

4 Est-ce que la Suisse est au sud de l'Italie?

5 Est-ce qu'il y a un centre commercial dans cette ville?

6 Est-ce qu'il y a une usine près de l'autoroute?

7 Est-ce qu'il y a un hôpital dans ce quartier?

8 Compléter: Dans une piscine, …

9 Compléter: Dans un centre commercial, …

10 Compléter: Dans un édifice, …

11 Compléter: Dans un musée, …

12 Compléter: Dans un hôtel, …

13 Compléter: Dans un cinéma, …

14 Compléter: Dans un distributeur de billets, …

15 Compléter: Dans une bibliothèque, …

16 Compléter: Dans un parc, …

17 Compléter: Dans une vidéo…

18 Compléter: Sur un pont, …

Réponses typiques

1 La France est loin des Etats-Unis.

2 L'Espagne est près de la France.

3 La Belgique est à côté du Luxembourg.

4 Non, la Suisse est au nord de l'Italie.

5 Oui, il y a un centre commercial dans cette ville.

6 Oui, il y a une usine près de l'autoroute.

7 Non, il n'y a pas d'hôpital dans ce quartier.

8 Dans une piscine, il y a de l'eau.

9 Dans un centre commercial, il y a des magasins.

10 Dans un édifice, il y a souvent des bureaux.

11 Dans un musée, les visiteurs regardent des tableaux.

12 Dans un hôtel, il y a des chambres.

13 Dans un cinéma, les spectateurs regardent l'écran.

14 Dans un distributeur, il y a de l'argent.

15 Dans une bibliothèque, les gens étudient.

16 Dans un parc, il y a des enfants.

17 Dans une vidéo, il y a des acteurs.

18 Sur un pont, il y a des voitures.

Histoire/Géographie 15

Online Search

A. Name (in French) the five countries where there is the greatest number of native English speakers.

① _____

② _____

③ _____

④ _____

⑤ _____

B. Name (in French) the five countries where there is the greatest number of native Spanish speakers.

① _____

② _____

③ _____

④ _____

⑤ _____

C. Name (in French) the five countries where there is the greatest number of native French speakers.

① _____

② _____

③ _____

④ _____

⑤ _____

D. How many people in the world speak English? _____

Spanish? _____ French? _____

E. Name (in French) the continents where French is spoken as a native language. _____

_____

Master List of Questions

Lesson 1

1. Salut. Ça va ?
2. Bonjour. Comment allez-vous?
3. Comment vous appelez-vous?
4. Je m'appelle Dominique. Et vous?
5. Au revoir, Claude.
6. Bien, merci. Et vous?
7. A bientôt.
8. Un plus quatre?
9. Trois plus six?
10. Deux plus cinq?
11. Cinq plus trois?
12. Six plus quatre?

Lesson 2

1. Deux plus cinq?
2. Quatre plus six?
3. Huit plus un?
4. Trois plus huit?
5. Neuf plus sept?
6. Onze plus trois?
7. Quatre plus quatorze?
8. Douze plus cinq?
9. Un plus quinze?
10. Dix-neuf plus un?
11. Normal ou pas normal: un mot dans un dictionnaire?
12. Normal ou pas normal: un parapluie au-dessus d'une personne?
13. Normal ou pas normal: un sol sur une montre?
14. Normal ou pas normal: une liste dans une lumière?

15. Normal ou pas normal: une horloge dans une salle de classe?
16. Normal ou pas normal: une corbeille à papier près d'un mur?
17. Normal ou pas normal: une chaise dans une carte?
18. Normal ou pas normal: des pages dans un livre?
19. Normal ou pas normal: un clavier sous un ordinateur.
20. Normal ou pas normal: une fenêtre derrière des rideaux?

Lesson 3

1. Vingt moins douze?
2. Treize moins sept?
3. Dix-neuf moins deux?
4. Dix-huit moins sept.
5. Seize moins six?
6. Quinze plus cinq?
7. Huit moins sept?
8. Dix-sept moins un?
9. Normal ou pas normal: un trombone dans un tiroir?
10. Normal ou pas normal: un secrétaire sous un tableau d'affichage?
11. Normal ou pas normal: un écran derrière un mur?
12. Normal ou pas normal: un employé dans un fauteuil?
13. Normal ou pas normal: une clé sous un fauteuil?

14. Normal ou pas normal: une souris dans une tasse?
15. Normal ou pas normal: des devoirs dans une bouteille.

Lesson 4

1. Il y a un tableau d'affichage sur des notes?
2. Il y a des tiroirs dans un trombone?
3. Il y a une salle de classe dans une chaise?
4. Il y a un bureau sous des enveloppes?
5. Il y a un sac à dos dans une clé?
6. Il y a une souris dans un clavier?
7. Il y a une table sur une tasse?
8. Il y a un bureau dans un patron?
9. Tu es d'où?
10. Il y a des étagères sur un dictionnaire?
11. Lundi est le premier jour de la semaine?
12. Mercredi est le deuxième jour de la semaine?
13. Jeudi est le troisième jour de la semaine?
14. Excusez-moi de vous déranger.
15. Quoi de neuf?
16. Le week-end est mardi et dimanche?

Lesson 5

1. Où y a-t-il des livres?
2. Où y a-t-il un réveil?
3. Où y a-t-il un journal?
4. Où y a-t-il une couverture?
5. Où y a-t-il une affiche?
6. Où y a-t-il des lampes?
7. Où y a-t-il un tapis?
8. Où y a-t-il des étudiants?
9. Où y a-t-il des vêtements?
10. Où y a-t-il des clés?
11. Où y a-t-il un tiroir?
12. Où y a-t-il un tableau?
13. Il y a une table sur la fenêtre?
14. Il y a des chambres dans la souris?
15. Comment est la télévision?

Lesson 6

1. Où est la clé?
2. Où sont les pantoufles?
3. Où est la salle de bains?

4. Il y a des fleurs ou des crayons dans le tiroir?
5. Il y a une, deux ou trois personnes dans la réunion?
6. Il y a une valise dans une calculatrice?
7. Il y a des étagères au-dessus de la commode?
8. Comment est ton lit?
9. Comment est ton chat?
10. Une poupée est un jouet ou un meuble?
11. J'adore le matin. Vous aussi?
12. Je déteste le parfum. Vous aussi?
13. Tu détestes quel jour?
14. Dix-huit moins onze font neuf?
15. Vingt-trois moins deux font vingt?

Lesson 7

1. Y a-t-il une poubelle derrière votre maison?
2. Y a-t-il une salle à manger au rez-de-chaussée chez vous?
3. Y a-t-il une salle de bain au premier étage chez vous?
4. Y a-t-il deux chambres chez vous?
5. Où y a-t-il des objets d'art chez vous?
6. Où est votre chambre?
7. Où est votre argent?
8. Où est le couloir chez vous?
9. Y a-t-il des toilettes près de votre chambre?
10. Y a-t-il une terrasse dans votre jardin?
11. Où est votre sac à dos?
12. Y a-t-il treize mois?
13. Y a-t-il huit jours dans une semaine?
14. Trente-neuf moins huit font vingt et un?
15. Dix-neuf plus huit font vingt-cinq?

Lesson 8

1. Vous avez des chiens?
2. On est au premier étage?
3. Vous êtes près de moi ou loin de moi?
4. Vous avez un réveil dans votre chambre?
5. Vos parents ont trois enfants?
6. Votre maison est dans un quartier résidentiel?

7. Je suis votre professeur?
8. Vous avez de la chance?
9. Bon courage!
10. Vous avez un camarade de chambre?
11. On est dans une salle de classe?
12. Quels sont les sept jours de la semaine?
13. Votre patron a quinze employés?
14. Je suis sur un banc?
15. Il y a des arbres dans votre jardin?
16. Le dîner est à quatre heures?
17. Le déjeuner est à dix heures?

Lesson 9

1. Vous aimez vos grands-parents ou vos enfants?
2. Vous détestez les légumes ou les fruits?
3. Vous aimez le vin français ou italien?
4. Votre famille a une ou deux voitures?
5. Votre mère aime les desserts ou les entrées?
6. Votre salle à manger a des tableaux ou des objets d'art?
7. Quels sont les douze mois de l'année?
8. Vous avez de l'eau dans votre sac à dos aujourd'hui?
9. Récitez l'alphabet, s'il vous plaît.
10. Un fauteuil est un meuble ou un vêtement?
11. Un facteur est une personne ou une chose?
12. Un cahier est une personne ou une chose?
13. Un voisin est une personne ou une chose?
14. Où y a-t-il du courrier?
15. Où y a-t-il de l'eau?

Lesson 10

1. Vous mangez vos légumes?
2. Vous aimez le poivre et le sel sur votre viande?
3. Vous achetez des repas à l'université?
4. Vous utilisez des baguettes ou une fourchette?
5. Vous lavez votre chien?
6. Vous regardez la télévision ou écoutez la radio?
7. Vous montrez des photos à une personne?
8. Vous donnez des documents à votre professeur?

9. Où rangez-vous vos couteaux?
10. Où regardez-vous un DVD?
11. Vous avez des bougies sur votre table de nuit?
12. Vous utilisez une serviette au restaurant?
13. Vous recommandez des émissions?
14. Où avez-vous des décorations?
15. Quelle est la date de votre anniversaire?

Lesson 11

1. Vous êtes jeune ou vieux/vieille ?
2. Vous êtes marié(e) ou célibataire ?
3. Les enfants vont à l'école dimanche?
4. Où allez-vous aujourd'hui?
5. Votre-grand mère est la soeur de votre grand-père?
6. Comment s'appelle votre mère?
7. Quelle est la date aujourd'hui?
8. Vingt plus cinquante-deux?
9. Quarante plus cinquante et un?
10. Vous allez à votre boîte aux lettres?
11. Vous avez votre portefeuille?
12. Votre oncle est le fils de votre père?
13. Vous apportez du thé à votre grand-mère?
14. Vos parents vont au supermarché aujourd'hui?

Lesson 12

1. Quel âge avez-vous?
2. Comment sont les vieillards?
3. Comment sont les bébés?
4. Comment sont les conducteurs?
5. Quelle sorte de magazines aimez-vous?
6. Quelle sorte d'idées avez-vous?
7. Quelle sorte de personnes détestez-vous?
8. Une piétonne est un homme ou une femme?
9. Un cuisinier est un homme ou une femme?
10. Votre famille habite dans une maison ou un appartement?
11. Qu'est-ce que vous achetez?
12. Qu'est-ce que vous transportez?
13. Qu'est-ce que vous organisez?
14. Qu'est-ce que vous terminez?

15. Qu'est-ce qu'un serveur apporte?
16. Qu'est-ce qu'un visiteur regarde?

Lesson 13

1. Vous voulez un peu de dessert?
2. Vous achetez quelques chaussures ou beaucoup de chaussures?
3. Vous écoutez un peu de musique dans votre voiture?
4. Quel âge ont tes parents?
5. Vous mangez un tas de fromage ou un peu de fromage?
6. Vous avez beaucoup de valises?
7. Qu'est-ce qu'il y a devant un barman?
8. Qu'est-ce qu'il y a devant un étudiant?
9. Qu'est-ce qu'il y a devant des spectateurs?
10. Qu'est-ce qu'il y a devant un enfant?
11. Qu'est-ce qu'il y a devant un petit ami?
12. Qu'est-ce qu'il y a devant un professeur?
13. Qu'est-ce qu'il y a devant un conducteur?
14. Comment est un chanteur?
15. Comment est un imbécile?
16. Comment est un pompier?
17. Comment est une citadine?
18. Comment est un barman?
19. Comment est une cycliste?
20. Comment est un fermier?

Lesson 14

1. Vous parlez souvent ou rarement?
2. Vous visitez souvent ou rarement un musée?
3. Vous utilisez tout le temps ou jamais le trottoir?
4. On va à l'église quel jour?
5. Vous achetez parfois ou souvent de la viande?
6. Vous skiez souvent ou rarement?
7. Vous travaillez souvent à la bibliothèque?

8. Combien de grands-parents avez-vous?
9. Il y a une quincaillerie dans votre quartier?
10. Où est votre supermarché?
11. Combien de classes avez-vous ce semestre?
12. Vous transportez souvent vos amis?
13. Qu'est-ce que vous réparez?
14. Vous insultez les gens?
15. Où allez-vous rarement?
16. Vous organisez parfois des fêtes?
17. Vous utilisez souvent une planche à pain?
18. Où dînez-vous souvent?

Lesson 15

1. Est-ce que la France est loin des Etats-Unis ou loin de l'Italie?
2. Est-ce que l'Espagne est près de la France ou près du Canada?
3. Est-ce que la Belgique est à côté du Luxembourg ou de l'Espagne?
4. Est-ce que la Suisse est au sud de l'Italie?
5. Est-ce qu'il y a un centre commercial dans cette ville?
6. Est-ce qu'il y a une usine près de l'autoroute?
7. Est-ce qu'il y a un hôpital dans ce quartier?
8. Compléter: Dans une piscine …
9. Compléter: Dans un centre commercial …
10. Compléter: Dans un édifice, …
11. Compléter: Dans un musée, …
12. Compléter: Dans un hôtel, …
13. Compléter: Dans un cinéma, …
14. Compléter: Dans un distributeur de billets, …
15. Compléter: Dans une bibliothèque, …
16. Compléter: Dans un parc, …
17. Compléter: Dans une vidéo, …
18. Compléter: Sur un pont, …

Dictionary
English-French

a *un(e) m./f.*
above *au-dessus de*
absent *absent(e)*
absolute *absolu(e)*
absolutely *en effet*
accept *accepter*
across from *en face de*
actor *acteur m.*
actress *actrice f.*
admire *admirer*
adorable *adorable*
affectionate *chaleureux/se*
again *encore*
age *âge m.*
aggressive *agressif/ive*
alarm clock *réveil m.*
all the time *tout le temps*
also *aussi*
always *toujours*
amazing *extraordinaire*
American *américain(e)*
an *un(e) m./f.*
and *et*
answer *réponse f.*
apartment *appartement m.*
appetizer *entrée f.*
appointment book *agenda m.*
appreciate *apprécier*
April *avril m.*
armchair *fauteuil m.*
arrive *arriver*
artist *artiste m./f.*

ask *demander* **ask for** *demander* **ask a question** *poser une question*
assignment *devoir m.*
at *à* **at my place** *chez moi* **at your place** *chez toi/vous*
athlete *athlète m./f.*
athletic *sportif/ive*
ATM machine *distributeur de billets m.*
audience member *spectateur/trice m./f.*
August *août m.*
author *auteur m.*
avancer *to progress, advance*
average (adj) *moyen/nne*
baby *bébé m./f.*
backpack *sac à dos m.*
bad *mauvais(e)*
badly *mal*
bag *sac m.*
bakery *pâtisserie f.*
bank *banque f.*
bartender *barman m.*
bathrobe *robe de chambre f.*
be able to *pouvoir*
beautiful *beau/belle*
be *être* **be lucky** *avoir de la chance*
bed *lit m.*
bedroom *chambre f.*
bedside table *table de nuit f.*
beer *bière f.*
begin *commencer*
behind *derrière*

beige *beige m.*
bench *banc m.*
beside *à côté de*
between *entre*
beverage *boisson f.*
big *grand(e)*
bike rider *cycliste m./f.*
birthday *anniversaire m.*
black (noun) *noir m.;* *noir(e)* (adj.)
blanket *couverture f.*
blue (noun) *bleu m.; bleu(e)* (adj.)
board *tableau* **bulletin board** *tableau d'affichage m.* **cutting board** *planche à pain f.*
book *livre m.*
bookstore *librairie f.*
boring *ennuyeux/se*
boss *patron/nne m./f.*
bother *déranger*
bottle *bouteille f.*
bowl *bol m.*
box *boîte f.*
boy *garçon* **boy friend** *petit ami m.*
brave *courageux/se*
bread *pain m.*
break (verb) *casser*
breakfast *petit déjeuner m.*
bridge *pont m.*
brillant *brillant(e)*
bring *apporter*
brother *frère m.*

brown (noun) *brun; brun(e)* (adj.)

building *édifice m.*

bulletin board *tableau d'affichage*

businessman *homme d'affaires*

businesswoman *femme d'affaires*

busy *occupé(e)*

butcher shop *boucherie f.*

butter *beurre m.*

buy *acheter*

bye *salut, ciao*

café *café m.*

calculator *calculatrice f.*

calendar *calendrier m.*

can (noun) *boîte f.; pouvoir* (verb)

Canadian *canadien/nne*

candle *bougie f.*

car *voiture f.*

card *carte f.*

carry *porter*

cat *chat m.*

cathedral *cathédrale f.*

cellar *cave f.*

cellphone *mobile m.*

center of town *centre-ville m.*

chair *chaise f.*

change *monnaie f.*

charming *charmant(e)*

chatty *bavard(e)*

cheese *fromage m.*

cheese shop *fromagerie f.*

chef *cuisinier/ère m./f.*

chick *meuf f.*

child *enfant m./f.*

china cabinet *buffet m.*

Chinese *chinois(e)*

chopstick *baguette f.*

church *église f.*

ciao *ciao*

city *ville f.*

city dweller *citadin(e) m./f.*

classroom *salle de classe f.*

clean (adj.) *propre* **clean up** (verb) *ranger*

cleaning woman *femme de ménage f.*

client *client(e) m./f.*

climb *grimper*

clock *horloge f.*

close (verb) *fermer*

closed *fermé(e)*

closet *placard m.*

clothes *vêtements m. pl.* **piece of clothing** *vêtement m.*

coffee *café m.*

coffee break *pause café f.*

cold *froid(e)*

cold cuts *charcuterie f.*

colleague *collègue m./f.*

come *venir* **to have just** (done something) *venir de*

comfortable *confortable*

communicate *communiquer*

competent *compétent(e)*

computer *ordinateur m.*

consult *consulter*

continue *continuer*

cook *cuisinier/ère m./f.*

copy (verb) *copier*

corner *coin m.*

couch *canapé m.*

courageous *courageux/se*

cup *tasse f.* **cup of coffee** *tasse de café*

cupboard *placard m.*

curtains *rideaux m. pl.*

customer *client(e) m./f.*

cut (verb) *couper*

cute *mignon/nne*

cutting board *planche à pain f.*

cyclist *cycliste m./f.*

dance (verb) *danser*

dancer *danseur/se m./f.*

dark (colored) *foncé(e)*

dark brown *brun m.* **brown-haired, brunette** *brun(e)*

date *date f.*

daughter *fille f.* **only daughter** *fille unique*

day *jour, journée f.* **have a good day** *bonne journée*

dead *mort(e)*

December *décembre m.*

decide *décider*

deck *terrasse f.*

decoration *décoration f.*

deli *charcuterie f.*

delicious *délicieux/se*

dentist *dentiste m./f.*

desk *bureau m.*

dessert *dessert m.*

develop *développer*

devoted *dévoué(e)*

dictionary *dictionnaire m.*

dinner *dîner m.* **eat dinner** *dîner* (verb)

director (movie) *réalisateur/trice m./f.*

dish *assiette f.* **main dish** *plat principal m.*

distribute *distribuer*

document *document m.*

dog *chien m.*

doll *poupée f.*

door *porte f.*

drawer *tiroir m.*

dream *rêve m.*

dressed *habillé(e)* **well dressed** *bien habillé(e)*

dresser *commode f.*

dressing *sauce f.*

drink *boisson f.*

driver *conducteur/trice*

dude *mec m.*

DVD *DVD m.*

east *est m.*

eat *manger* **eat dinner** *dîner*

egotistical *égoïste*

elderly person *vieillard m.*

electricity *électricité f.*
elegant *élégant(e)*
employee *employé(e) m./f.*
end (verb) *finir*
energetic *énergique*
engineer *ingénieur m.*
enter *entrer*
entertaining *divertissant(e)*
enthusiastic *enthousiaste*
envelope *enveloppe f.*
evening *soir m.*
exam *examen m.*
examine *examiner*
excellent *excellent(e)*
excuse me *excusez-moi, pardon*
expensive *cher/chère*
experienced *expérimenté(e)*
extraordinary *extraordinaire*
facing *en face de*
factory *usine f.*
fairly *assez*
family *famille f.*
famous *célèbre*
fancy *élégant(e)*
fantastic *magnifique, formidable*
far from *loin de*
farmer *fermier/ère*
fashion designer *styliste m./f.*
fast *rapide*
fat *gros/sse*
father *père*
February *février m.*
filmmaker *réalisateur/trice m./f.*
find (verb) *trouver*
fine *ça va (= I am fine.)*
finish *terminer*
fireman *pompier m.*
fireplace *cheminée f.*
first *premier/ère*
fish *poisson m.*
fix *réparer*

floor (of building) *étage m.; sol m.* (under foot)
flower *fleur f.*
fork *fourchette f.*
fourth *quatrième*
frame *cadre m.*
freeway *autoroute f.*
French *français(e)*
Friday *vendredi m.* **on Friday** *vendredi* **on Fridays** *le vendredi*
friend *ami(e) m./f.* **boyfriend** *petit ami m.* **girlfriend** *petite amie f.*
friendly *sympa, sympathique*
from *de, d'* **from here** *d'ici* **from the** *du, de la, de l', des* **from where** *d'où*
fruit *fruit m.*
fun *amusant(e)*
furniture *meubles m. pl.* **piece of furniture** *meuble m.*
garage *garage m.* **mechanic** *garagiste m./f.*
garden *jardin m.*
generous *généreux/se*
get home *rentrer*
girl *fille f.* **girl friend** *petite amie f.*
give *donner*
glad *content(e)* **glad to meet you** *enchanté(e)*
glass *verre m.* **wine glass** *verre à vin m.* **glass of wine** *verre de vin m.*
glasses *lunettes f. pl.* **sunglasses** *lunettes de soleil*
go *aller* **go back** *retourner* **go in** *entrer*
good *bon/bonne* **good afternoon** *bonjour* **good morning** *bonjour* **have a good day** *bonne journée*
goodbye *au revoir*

gray (noun) *gris m.; gris(e)* (adj.)
green (noun) *vert m.; vert(e)* (adj.)
grocery store (small) *épicerie f.*
ground floor *rez-de-chaussée m.*
guitar *guitare f.*
hair stylist *coiffeur/se m./f.*
half *demi(e) m./f.*
hall *couloir m.*
hallway *couloir m.*
happy *content(e)*
hardware store *quincaillerie f.*
hardworking *travailleur/se*
have *avoir* **have a good day** *bonne journée*
have to *devoir*
he *il* **he is** *c'est, elle est, il est*
hello *bonjour;* (on the phone only) *allô*
her *son, sa, ses*
here *ici, là*
hi *salut*
high school *lycée m.*
high-energy *énergique*
highway *autoroute f.*
his *son, sa, ses*
holiday *fête f.*
homework *devoirs m.*
hospital *hôpital m.*
hotel *hôtel m.*
hour *heure f.*
house *maison f.*
housekeeper *femme de ménage f.*
houseplant *plante verte f.*
how *comment* **how are you?** *ça va?, comment allez-vous? comment vas-tu?*
huge *énorme*
I *je*
ice cube *glaçon m.*
idea *idée f.*
idiot *imbécile m./f.*

ill *malade*
impatient *impatient(e)*
impressed *impressionné(e)*
Impressionist *impressioniste*
improve *améliorer*
in *dans* **in a hurry** *pressé(e)* **in between** *entre* **in front of** *devant* **in love** *amoureux/se*
indeed *en effet*
innovative *innovateur/trice*
insult (verb) *insulter*
intelligent *intelligent(e)*
intense *intense*
interested *intéressé(e)*
interesting *intéressant(e)*
into *dans*
invite *inviter*
invent *inventer*
is *est* **isn't** *n'est pas* **isn't that true?** *n'est-ce pas?*
it *ça, ce, il, elle* **it is** *c'est, elle est, il est*
Italian *italien/nne*
January *janvier m.*
jewelry *bijoux m.pl.*
jewels *bijoux m.pl.*
job *job m.*
July *juillet m.*
June *juin*
keep *garder*
key *clé f.*
keyboard *clavier m.*
knife *couteau m.* **knives** *couteaux*
know *savoir*
laborer *ouvrier/ère m./f.*
lamp *lampe f.*
laptop *laptop m.*
large *grand(e)*
laundry *linge m.*
leave (verb) *quitter*
lecturer *conférencier/ère m./f.*
left *gauche* **on the left** (of) *à gauche (de)*
lesson *leçon f.*

letter *lettre f.*
library *bibliothèque f.*
light (noun) *lumière f.* **light** (colored) *clair(e)* (adj.)
like (verb) *aimer bien*
list *liste f.*
listen *écouter* **listen to** *écouter*
little *petit(e)*
live *habiter*
loaf of bread *baguette f.*
look (verb) *regarder* **look at** *regarder* **look for** *chercher*
lots of *beaucoup de, un tas de*
love (verb) *adorer, aimer*
lovely *beau/belle*
luck *chance f.* **to be lucky** *avoir de la chance*
lunch *déjeuner m.*
magazine *magazine m.*
magnificent *magnifique*
mail *courrier m.*
mailbox *boîte aux lettres f.*
mailman *facteur m.*
main course *plat principal m.*
make *faire* **make up** *inventer*
mall *centre commercial m.*
man *homme m.*
map *carte f.*
March *mars m.*
market *marché m.*
married *marié(e)*
May *mai m.*
maybe *peut-être*
me *moi*
meal *repas m.*
meat *viande f.*
meeting *réunion f.*
member *membre m./f.*
menu *carte f.*
message *message m.*
messenger *messager/ère m./f.*
meter *mètre m.*
Mexican *mexicain(e)*
mirror *miroir m.*
Monday *lundi m.*

money *argent m.*
month *mois m.*
monument *monument m.*
morning *matin m.*
moron *imbécile m./f.*
mother *mère f.*
mouse *souris f.*
movie *film m.*
mp3 player *lecteur mp3 m.*
movie director *réalisateur/trice*
movie theater *cinéma m.*
museum *musée m.*
music *musique f.*
must *devoir*
my *mon, ma, mes* **my name is** *je m'appelle*
mysterious *mystérieux/se*
napkin *serviette f.*
natural *naturel/lle*
near *près de*
need *avoir besoin de*
neighbor *voisin(e) m./f.*
neighborhood *quartier m.* **residential neighorhood** *quartier residentiel*
never *ne (+ verb +) jamais*
new *nouveau/elle* **brand new** *neuf/ve*
newspaper *journal m.*
next to *à côté de*
nice *sympa, agréable*
night *nuit f.*
night table *table de nuit f.*
nightclub *boîte de nuit f.*
no *non*
north *nord m.*
not *pas*
note *note f.*
notebook *cahier m.*
nothing *rien*
November *novembre m.*
nombre *number m.*
nurse *infirmier/ère m./f.*
o'clock *heure f.*

object *objet m.*
observe *observer*
October *octobre m.*
of *de, d'* **of the** *du, de la, de l',*
    des **of course!** *bien sûr!*
office *bureau m.*
often *souvent*
oh really? *ah bon?*
OK *d'accord, OK*
old *ancien/nne, vieux/vieille*
on *sur*
    on Monday(s) *(le) lundi*
    on Tuesday(s) *(le) mardi*
    on Wednesday(s)
    (le) mercredi
    on Thursday(s) *(le) jeudi*
    on Friday(s) *(le) vendredi*
    on Saturday(s) *(le) samedi*
    on Sunday(s) *(le) dimanche*
one (number) *un(e) m./f.* ; *on*
    (pronoun)
open *ouvert(e)*
or *ou*
orange (color) *orange m.; f.*
    (fruit)
order (verb) *commander*
ordinary *ordinaire*
organize *organiser*
other *autre*
our *notre, nos*
page *page f.*
painting *tableau m.*
pan *poêle f.*
paper *papier m.*
paperclip *trombone m.*
parent *parent m.*
park *parc m.*
participant *participant(e) m./f.*
party *fête f.*
pass (verb) *passer*
passenger *passager/ère m./f.*
patient *patient(e)*
patio *terrasse f.*
pedestrian *piéton/nne m./f.*
pen *stylo m.*
pencil *crayon m.*

people *gens m. pl.*
pepper *poivre m.*
perfume *parfum m.*
perhaps *peut-être*
person *personne f.*
pharmacy *pharmacie f.*
photo *photo f.*
piece of clothing *vêtement*
    m. **clothes** *vêtements m. pl.*
piece of furniture *meuble m.*
piece of paper *feuille de*
    papier f.
pillow *oreiller m.*
pink (noun) *rose m.* **pink** *rose*
    (adj.)
pitcher *carafe f.*
place (verb) *placer*
place setting *couvert m.*
plate *assiette f.*
player *joueur/se m./f.*
plaza *place f.*
pleasant *agréable*
please *s'il vous plaît*
police station *préfecture de*
    police f.
policeman *policier m.*
poor *pauvre*
poorly *mal*
postal carrier *facteur m.*
poster *affiche f.*
pot *casserole f.*
prefer *préférer*
prepare *préparer*
pretty *joli(e)*
printer *imprimante f.*
problem *problème m.*
professor *professeur m.*
psychologist *psychologue m./f.*
pure *pure*
purple (noun) *violet m.*
    violet/tte (adj.)
put away *ranger*
question *question f.*
quiet *tranquille, silencieux/se*
radio *radio f.*

rarely *rarement*
rather *assez*
real *vrai(e)*
recipe *recette f.*
recommander *to recommend*
red *rouge m.*
refuse (verb) *refuser*
regret (verb) *regretter*
rent (verb) *louer*
repair (verb) *réparer*
repeat *répéter*
residential *résidentiel/lle*
respect (verb) *respecter*
response *réponse f.*
restaurant *restaurant m.*
restroom *toilettes f.pl.*
return *retourner (to a place)*
rich *riche*
right *droite f.* **on the right**
    (of) *à droite (de)* **right?**
    n'est-ce pas?
road *route f.*
roof *toit m.*
room *pièce f., salle f.*
    diningroom *salle à manger*
    f. **bathroom** *salle de bains*
    f. **roommate** *camarade de*
    chambre m./f. **livingroom**
    salle de séjour f.
rug *tapis m.*
rushed *pressé(e)*
Russian *russe*
salad *salade f.*
salesman *vendeur m.*
saleswoman *vendeuse f.*
salt *sel m.*
Saturday *samedi m.* **on**
    Saturday *samedi* **on**
    Saturdays *le samedi*
sauce *sauce f.*
school *école f.*
scientist *scientifique m./f.*
screen *écran m.*
seat *place f.*
second *deuxième*
secretary *secrétaire m./f.*

see you later *à tout à l'heure*
see you soon *à bientôt*
see you tomorrow *à demain*
selfish *égoïste*
senior citizen *vieillard m.*
September *septembre m.*
serious *grave, sérieux/se*
server *serveur/se m./f.*
she *elle*
sheet of paper *feuille de papier f.*
she is *c'est, elle est*
shelf *étagère f.*
shoe *chaussure f.*
show (TV) *émission f.* **show** (verb) *montrer*
sick *malade*
side *côté m.*
sideboard *buffet m.*
sidewalk *trottoir m.*
silent *silencieux/se*
sing *chanter*
singer *chanteur/se m./f.*
single *célibataire*
sister *soeur f.*
ski (verb) *skier*
skillet *poêle f.*
skyscraper *gratte-ciel m.*
slim *mince*
slipper *pantoufle f.*
small *petit(e)*
smart *intelligent(e)*
sofa *canapé m.*
solar panel *panneau solaire m.*
some *du, de la, de l', des*
sometimes *parfois*
son *fils m.* **only son** *fils unique*
soon *bientôt*
sorry *pardon, excusez-moi*
south *sud m.*
speak *parler* **to** *à* **about** *de*
spectator *spectateur/trice m./f.*
spoon *cuillère f.*
sports field *terrain de sport m.*
square (in town) *place f.*

stadium *stade m.*
stairs *escalier m.*
stairway *escalier m.*
start *commencer*
stationery store *papéterie f.*
stay *rester*
stereo *chaîne stéréo f.*
Steven *Etienne m.*
still *encore*
store *magasin m.*
stove *cuisinière*
straight ahead *tout droit*
street *rue f.*
strong *fort(e)*
student (college) *étudiant(e) m./f.*
student (pre-college) *élève m./f.*
study *étudier*
stupid *bête* **stupid person** *imbecile m./f.*
sugar *sucre m.*
suitcase *valise f.*
sun *soleil m.*
Sunday *dimanche m.* **on Sunday** *dimanche* **on Sundays** *le dimanche*
sunglasses *lunettes de soleil f.*
supermarket *supermarché m.*
swimming pool *piscine f.*
table *table f.* **bedside table** *table de nuit*
tablecloth *nappe f.*
tablet *tablette f.*
talented *talentueux/se*
talk *parler* **to** *à* **about** *de*
talkative *bavard(e)*
tall *grand(e)*
tea *thé m.*
teacher *professeur m.*
telephone *téléphone m.*
television *télévision f.*
terrace *terrasse f.*
test *examen m.*
thank you *merci* **thanks very much** *merci beaucoup* **thanks a lot** *merci bien*

thanks *merci*
that's right *c'est ça*
the *le, la, l', les*
theater *théâtre m.*
their *leur, leurs*
there *là*
there is, there are *il y a* **there is/are no...** *il n'y a pas de...*
there's...! there are...! *voilà...!*
these *ces*
they *elles, ils*
thin *mince*
thing *chose f.*
think *penser* **about** *à* **that** *que*
third *troisième*
this (pronoun) *ça* **this** (adj) *ce, cet, cette* **this is** *c'est, elle est, il est*
Thursday *jeudi* **on Thursday** *jeudi* **on Thursdays** *le jeudi*
time *heure f.* **all the time** *tout le temps*
tiny *minuscule*
tired *fatigué(e)*
to *à*
today *aujourd'hui*
together *ensemble*
tomorrow *demain*
tonight *ce soir*
touch (verb) *toucher*
toy *jouet m.*
train station *gare f.*
transport (verb) *transporter*
trashcan *poubelle f.*
tray *plateau m.*
tree *arbre m.*
true *vrai(e)*
Tuesday *mardi m.* **on Tuesday** *mardi* **on Tuesdays** *le mardi*
turn *tourner* (verb)
TV program *émission f.*
TV viewer *téléspectateur/trice m./f.*

typical *typique*

ugly *moche*

umbrella *parapluie m.*

uncomfortable *inconfortable*

under *sous*

understanding *compréhensif/ive* (adj.)

unexpected *inattendu(e)*

university *université f.*, **fac** *f.*

unmarried *célibataire*

urbanite *citadin(e) m./f.*

usually *d'habitude*

use (verb) *utiliser*

useful *utile*

vase *vase m.*

vegetable *légume m.*

very *très* **very much** *beaucoup* **very sorry** *désolé(e)*

victorious *victorieux/se*

video *vidéo f.*

view *vue f.*

visit (verb) *visiter*

visitor *visiteur/se m./f.*

wait *patienter*

walk (verb) *marcher*

wall *mur m.*

wallet *portefeuille m.*

want *vouloir*

warm *chaleureux/se*

wash (verb) *laver*

wastebasket *corbeille à papier f.*

watch (noun) *montre f.* **watch** (verb) *regarder*

water *eau f.*

we *nous, on*

wear *porter*

Wednesday *mercredi m.* **on Wednesday** *mercredi* **on Wednesdays** *le mercredi*

week *semaine f.*

welcome *bienvenue* **you're welcome** *de rien, je vous/t'en prie, pas de quoi*

well *bien*

west *ouest m.*

What...? *Qu'est-ce que...?*

What time is it? *Quelle heure est-il?*

what's this/that/it? *qu'est-ce que c'est?*

where *où* **where is it** *où est-ce* **from where** *d'où*

which? *quel?, quelle?, quels?, quelles?*

white (noun) *blanc m.; blanc/blanche* (adj.)

why *pourquoi*

widowed *veuf/veuve*

wife *femme f.*

window *fenêtre f.*

winning *victorieux/se*

woman *femme f.*

word *mot m.*

work *travail m.* **work of art** *objet d'art m.* **work** (verb) *travailler*

worker *ouvrier/ère m./f.*

wristwatch *montre f.*

write *écrire*

yard *jardin m.*

yellow *jaune m.*

yes *oui*

you *toi, tu, vous*

you're welcome *de rien, je t'/vous en prie, pas de quoi*

young *jeune*

your *ton, ta, tes, votre, vos*

Dictionnaire
Français-Anglais

à *at, to, in* **à bientôt** *see you soon* **à demain** *see you tomorrow*
absent(e) *absent*
absolu(e) *absolute*
accepter *to accept*
acheter *to buy*
acteur/trice m./f. *actor*
adorable *adorable*
adorer *to love*
affiche f. *poster*
âge m. *age* **quel âge avez-vous?** *how old are you?*
agenda m. *appointment book*
agressif/ve *aggressive*
agréable *pleasant*
ah bon? *oh really?*
aimer *to love like* **aimer bien** *to like*
aller *to go*
allô *hello* (on the phone only)
améliorer *to improve*
américain(e) *American*
ami(e) m./f. *friend*
amoureux/se *in love*
amusant(e) *fun*
ancien/nne *old*
anniversaire m. *birthday*
août m. *August*
appartement m. *apartment*
apporter *to bring*
apprécier *appreciate*
arbre m. *tree*
argent m. *money*

arriver *to arrive*
artiste m./f. *artist*
assez *fairly, rather*
assiette f. *plate, dish*
athlète m./f. *athlete*
au revoir *goodbye*
au-dessus de *above*
aujourd'hui *today*
aussi *also, too*
auteur m. *author*
autoroute f. *freeway, highway*
autre *other*
avoir *to have* **avoir de la chance** *to be lucky* **avoir besoin de** *need* (verb)
avril m. *April*
baguette f. *loaf of bread, chopstick*
banc m. *bench*
banque f. *bank*
barman m. *bartender*
bavard(e) *chatty, talkative*
beau/belle *lovely, beautiful*
beaucoup *a lot, very much*
bébé m./f. *baby*
bière f. *beer*
beige m. *beige*
besoin m. *need* **avoir besoin de** *need* (verb)
bête *stupid*
beurre m. *butter*
bibliothèque f. *library*
bien *well, a lot*
bien sûr! *of course!*

bientôt *soon* **à bientôt** *see you soon*
bijoux m. pl. *jewelry, jewels*
blanc m. *white* **blanc/che** (adj.)
bleu m. *blue* **bleu(e)** (adj.)
boisson f. *beverage, drink*
boîte aux lettres f. *mailbox*
boîte de nuit f. *nightclub*
boîte f. *box, can*
bol m. *bowl*
bon/bonne *good* **bon courage** *good luck* **bonne journée** *have a good day*
bonjour *hello, good morning, good afternoon*
boucherie f. *butcher shop*
bougie f. *candle*
bouteille f. *bottle*
brillant(e) *brillant*
brun m. *dark brown* **brun(e)** (adj.) *brown-haired, brunette*
buffet m. *china cabinet, sideboard*
bureau m. *desk, office*
c'est *it is, this is, he is, she is* **c'est ça** *that's right*
ça *this, that* (pronoun) **ça va** *how's it going, fine*
cadre m. *frame*
café m. *coffee, café*
cahier m. *notebook*
calculatrice f. *calculator*
calendrier m. *calendar*

camarade de chambre m./f. *roommate*

canadien/nne *Canadian*

canapé m. *sofa, couch*

carafe f. *pitcher*

carte f. *map, card, menu*

casser *to break*

casserole f. *pot*

cathédrale f. *cathedral*

cave f. *cellar*

ce, cet, cette; ces *this; these*

célèbre *famous*

célibataire *single, unmarried*

centre commercial m. *mall*

centre-ville m. *the center of town*

certain(e) *certain*

chaîne stéréo f. *stereo*

chaise f. *chair*

chaleureux/se *(emotionally) warm, affectionate*

chambre f. *bedroom* **robe de chambre** f. *bathrobe*

chanter *to sing*

chanteur/se m./f. *singer*

charcuterie f. *deli, cold cuts*

charmant(e) *charming*

chat m. *cat*

chaussure f. *shoe*

cheminée f. *fireplace*

chercher *to look for*

chez moi *at my place*

chez toi/vous *at your place*

chien m. *dog*

chinois(e) *Chinese*

chose f. *thing*

ciao *ciao, bye*

cinéma m. *movie theater*

citadin (e) m./f. *city dweller, urbanite*

clair(e) *light* (colored)

clavier m. *keyboard*

clé f. *key*

client(e) m./f. *customer, client*

coiffeur/se m./f. *hair stylist*

coin m. *corner*

collègue m./f. *co-worker, colleague*

commander *to order*

commencer *to begin, start*

communiquer *to communicate*

comment *how* **comment ça va?** *how are you?* **comment allez-vous** *how are you?*

commode f. *dresser*

communiquer *to communicate*

compétent(e) *competent*

compréhensif/ive *understanding*

conducteur/trice m./f. *driver*

conférencier/ère m./f. *lecturer*

confortable *comfortable*

consulter *to consult, talk with*

content(e) *happy*

continuer *to continue*

copier *to copy*

corbeille à papier f. *wastebasket*

côté m. *side* **à côté de** *beside, next to*

couloir m. *hall, hallway*

couper *to cut*

courageux/se *brave, courageous*

courrier m. *mail*

couteau m. *knife* **couteaux** *knives*

couvert m. *place setting*

couverture f. *blanket*

crayon m. *pencil*

cuillère f. *spoon*

cuisine f. *kitchen*

cuisinier/ère *cook, chef*

cuisinière f. *stove*

cycliste m./f. *cyclist, bike rider*

d'accord *OK*

d'où *from where*

dans *in, into*

danser *to dance*

danseur/se m./f. *dancer*

date f. *date*

de rien *you're welcome*

de, d' *of, from* **d'accord** *OK*

d'où *from where* **d'ici** *from here* **de rien** *you're welcome*

décembre m. *December*

décider *to decide*

décoration f. *decoration*

déjeuner m. *lunch* **petit déjeuner** *breakfast*

délicieux/se *delicious*

demain *tomorrow* **à demain** *see you tomorrow*

demander *to ask, ask for*

demi(e) *half*

dentiste m./f. *dentist*

déranger *to bother*

derrière *behind*

désolé(e) *very sorry*

dessert m. *dessert*

devant *in front of*

développer *to develop*

devoir (verb) *must, have to* (sing. noun) *assignment* (plur. noun) *homework*

dévoué(e) *devoted*

d'habitude *usually*

dictionnaire m. *dictionary*

dimanche m. *Sunday, on Sunday* **le dimanche** *on Sundays*

dîner m. *dinner; to eat dinner* (verb)

distribuer *to distribute*

distributeur de billets m. *ATM machine*

divertissant(e) *entertaining*

document m. *document*

donner *to give*

droite f. *right* **à droite (de)** *on the right (of)*

du, de la, de l', des *some, of the, from the*

DVD m. *DVD*

eau f. *water*

école f. *school*

écouter *to listen, listen to*

écran m. *screen*

écrire *to write*

édifice m. *building*

église f. *church*

égoïste *selfish, egotistical*

électricité f. *electricity*

élégant(e) *fancy, elegant*

élève m./f. (pre-college) *student*

elle *she*

elles *they*

émission f. *TV program*

employé(e) m./f. *employee*

en effet *indeed*

en face de *facing, across from*

enchanté(e) *glad to meet you*

encore *still, again*

en effet *absolutely, indeed*

énergique *energetic, high-energy*

enfant m./f. *child*

ennuyeux/se *boring*

énorme *huge*

ensemble *together*

enthousiaste *enthusiastic*

entre *between, in between*

entrée f. *appetizer*

entrer *to enter*

enveloppe f. *envelope*

épicerie f. *neighborhood grocery store*

escalier m. *stairs, stairway*

est m. *east; is* (verb)

et *and*

étage m. *floor* (of building)

étagère f. *shelf*

Etienne m. *Steven*

être *to be*

étudiant(e) m./f. (college) *student*

étudier *to study*

examen m. *exam, test*

examiner *to examine*

excellent(e) *excellent*

excusez-moi *excuse me*

expérimenté(e) *experienced*

extraordinaire *extraordinary, amazing*

fac f. *university*

facteur m. *postal carrier*

famille f. *family*

fatigué(e) *tired*

fauteuil m. *armchair*

femme f. *woman, wife* **femme d'affaires** *business-woman* **femme de ménage** *cleaning woman, housekeeper*

fenêtre f. *window*

fermer *to close*

fermé(e) *closed*

fermier/ère m./f. *farmer*

fête f. *holiday, party*

feuille de papier f. *sheet of paper*

février m. *February*

fille f. *daughter, girl* **fille unique** f. *(female) only child*

film m. *film, movie*

fils m. *son* **fils unique** m. *(male) only child*

finir *to end, finish*

fleur f. *flower*

foncé(e) *dark* (colored)

formidable

fort(e) *strong, loud*

fourchette f. *fork*

français(e) *French*

frère m. *brother*

froid(e) (adj.) *cold*

fromage m. *cheese*

fromagerie f. *cheese shop*

fruit m. *fruit*

garage m. *garage*

garagiste m./f. *car mechanic*

garcon m. *boy*

garder *to keep*

gare f. *train station*

gauche f. *left* **à gauche (de)** *on the left (of)*

généreux/se *generous*

gens m. pl. *people*

glaçon m. *ice cube*

grand(e) *tall, large, big*

gratte-ciel m. *skyscraper*

grave *serious*

grimper *to climb*

gris(e) m. *gray*

gros/grosse *fat, big, large*

guitare f. *guitar*

habillé(e) *well dressed* **bien habillé(e)**

habiter *to live*

heure f. *time, hour, o'clock*

homme m. *man* **homme d'affaires** *businessman*

hôpital m. *hospital*

horloge f. *clock*

hotel m. *hotel*

ici *here*

idée f. *idea*

il *he, it*

il y a *there is, there are* **il n'y a pas de…** *there is/are no…*

ils *they*

imbécile m./f. *idiot, moron, stupid person*

impatient(e) *impatient*

impressionné(e) *impressed*

imprimante f. *printer*

inattendu(e) *unexpected*

inconfortable *uncomfortable*

infirmier/ère m./f. *nurse*

ingénieur m. *engineer*

innovateur/trice *innovative*

insulter *to insult*

intelligent(e) *intelligent, smart*

intense *intense*

intéressant(e) *interesting*

intéressé(e) *interested*

inventer *to invent, make up*

inviter *to invite*

italien/nne *Italian*

jamais *(ne…) never*

janvier m. *January*

jardin m. *yard, garden*

jaune m. *yellow*

je *I* **je m'appelle** *my name is*

je vous/t' en prie *you're welcome*

jeudi m. *Thursday, on Thursday* **le jeudi** *on Thursdays*

jeune *young*

job m. *job*

joli(e) *pretty*

jouet m. *toy*

joueur/se *player*

jour m. *day*

journal m. *newspaper*

journée f. *day* **bonne journée** *have a good day*

juillet m. *July*

juin m. *June*

là *here, there*

lampe f. *lamp*

laptop m. *laptop*

laver *to wash*

leçon f. *lesson*

lecteur mp3 m. *mp3 player*

le, la, l', les *the*

légume m. *vegetable*

lettre f. *letter*

librairie f. *bookstore*

linge m. *laundry*

liste f. *list*

lit m. *bed*

livre m. *book*

loin de *far from*

louer *to rent*

lumière f. *light*

lundi m. *Monday, on Monday* **le lundi** *on Mondays*

lunettes f. pl *glasses* **lunettes de soleil** f. pl. *sunglasses*

lycée m. *high school*

magasin m. *store*

magazine m. *magazine*

magnifique *fantastic, magnificent*

mai m. *May*

maison f. *house*

mal *badly, poorly*

malade *sick, ill*

manger *to eat*

marché m. *market*

marcher *to walk*

mardi m. *Tuesday, on Tuesday* le mardi *on Tuesdays*

marié(e) *married*

marron m. *brown;* **marron** *adj.*

mars m. *March*

matin m. *morning*

mauvais(e) *bad*

mec m. *"dude"*

membre m./f. *member*

merci *thank you, thanks* **merci beaucoup** *thanks very much* **merci bien** *thanks a lot*

mercredi m. *Wednesday, on Wednesday* le mercredi *on Wednesdays*

mère *mother*

message m. *message*

messager/ère m./f. *messenger*

mètre m. *meter*

meuble m. *piece of furniture* **meubles** m. pl. *furniture*

meuf f. *"chick"*

mexicain(e) *Mexican*

mignon/nne *cute*

mince *thin, slim*

minuscule *tiny*

miroir m. *mirror*

mobile m. *cellphone*

moche *ugly*

moi *me*

mois m. *month*

mon, ma, mes *my*

monnaie f. *change ($)*

montre f. *wristwatch*

montrer *to show*

monument m. *monument*

mort(e) *dead*

mot m. *word*

moyen/nne (adj) *average*

mur m. *wall*

musée m. *museum*

musique f. *music*

mystérieux/se *mysterious*

n'est-ce pas? *right? isn't that true?*

nappe f. *tablecloth*

naturel/lle *natural*

ne (+ verb +) pas *not*

neuf/ve *brand new*

noir(e) m. *black*

nombre m. *number*

non *no*

nord m. *north*

note f. *note*

nous *we*

nouveau/elle *new*

novembre m. *November*

nuit f. *night*

objet m. *object* **objet d'art** m. *work of art*

observer *to observe*

occupé(e) *busy*

octobre m. *October*

on *we, one*

orange m. *orange (color);* f. *(fruit)*

ordinaire *ordinary*

ordinateur m. *computer*

oreiller m. *pillow*

organiser *to organize*

ou *or*

où *where* **où est-ce** *where is it* **d'où** *from where*

ouest m. *west*

oui *yes*

ouvert(e) *open*

ouvrier/ère m./f. *worker, laborer*

page f. *page*

pain m. *bread*

panneau solaire m. *solar panel*

pantoufle f. *slipper*

papéterie f. *stationery store*

papier m. *paper*

parapluie m. *umbrella*

parc m. *park*

pardon *excuse me, sorry*

parent m. *parent*

parfois *sometimes*

parfum m. *perfume*

parler *to speak, talk* **à** *to* **de** *about*

participant(e) m./f. *participant*

pas *not*

passager/ère *passenger*

passer *to pass*

patient(e) *patient*

patienter *to wait*

patisserie f. *bakery*

patron/nne m./f. *boss*

pause café f. *coffee break*

pauvre *poor*

penser *to think* **à** *about* **que** *that*

père *father*

personne f. *person*

petit déjeuner m. *breakfast*

petit(e) *small, little* **petit(e) ami(e)** m./f. *boy/girl friend*

peut-être *maybe, perhaps*

pharmacie f. *pharmacy*

photo f. *photo*

pièce f. *room*

piéton/nne m./f. *pedestrian*

piscine f. *swimming pool*

placard m. *closet, cupboard*

place f. *seat, (town) square*

placer *to place*

planche à pain f. *cutting board*

plante verte f. *houseplant*

plat principal m. *main course*

plateau m. *tray*

poêle f. *pan, skillet*

poisson m. *fish*

poivre m. *pepper*

policier m. *policeman*

pompier m. *fireman*

pont m. *bridge*

porte f. *door*

portefeuille m. *wallet*

porter *to carry, wear*

poser une question *to ask a question*

poubelle f. *trashcan*

poupée f. *doll*

pourquoi *why*

pouvoir *to be able to, can*

préfecture de police f. *police station*

préférer *to prefer*

premier/ère *first*

préparer *to prepare*

près de *near*

pressé(e) *rushed, in a hurry*

problème m. *problem*

professeur m. *teacher, professor*

propre *clean*

psychologue m./f. *psychologist*

pure *pure*

qu'est-ce que c'est? *what's this/that?, what is it?*

quartier m. *neighborhood* **quartier residential** *residential neighorhood*

quel/lle? *which?* **Quelle heure est-il?** *What time is it?*

qu'est-ce que...? *What...?*

question f. *question*

quincaillerie f. *hardware store*

quitter *to leave*

radio f. *radio*

ranger *to put away, tidy up*

rapide *fast*

rarement *rarely*

réalisateur/trice m./f. *film maker, film director*

recette f. *recipe*

recommander *to recommend*

refuser *to refuse, turn down*

regarder *to watch, look, look at*

regretter *to regret*

rentrer *to go/get/come home*

réparer *to fix, repair*

repas m. *meal*

répéter *to repeat*

réponse f. *answer, response*

résidentiel/lle *residential*

respecter *to respect*

restaurant m. *restaurant*

rester *to stay*

retourner *to return, go back*

réunion f. *meeting*

rêve m. *dream*

réveil m. *alarm clock*

rez-de-chaussée m. *ground floor*

riche *rich*

rideaux m.pl. *curtains*

rien *nothing* **de rien** *you're welcome*

robe de chambre f. *bathrobe*

rose m. *pink;* f. *(flower)*

rouge *red*

route f. *road*

rue f. *street*

russe *Russian*

s'il vous plaît *please*

sac m. *bag* **sac à dos** m. *backpack*

salade f. *salad*

salle f. *room* **salle à manger** *diningroom* **salle de bains** *bathroom* **salle de classe** *classroom* **salle de séjour** *livingroom*

salut *hi, bye*

samedi m. *Saturday, on Saturday* **le samedi** *on Saturdays*

sauce f. *sauce, dressing*

savoir *to know*

scientifique m./f. *scientist*

secrétaire m./f. *secretary*

sel m. *salt*

semaine f. *week*

septembre m. *September*

sérieu<u>x/se</u> *serious*

serveu<u>r/se</u> m./f. *server*

serviette f. *napkin*

silencieux/se *silent, quiet*

skier *to ski*

soeur f. *sister*

soir m. *evening* **ce soir** *tonight*

sol m. *floor*

soleil m. *sun* **lunettes de soleil** *sunglasses*

souris f. *mouse*

sous *under*

souvent *often*

spectateur/trice m./f. *spectator, audience member*

sportif/ive *athletic*

stade m. *stadium*

stylo m. *pen*

sucre m. *sugar*

sud m. *south*

supermarché m. *supermarket*

sur *on*

syliste m./f. *fashion designer*

sympa *nice*

table de nuit f. *night table*

table f. *table*

tableau m. *board, painting* **tableau d'affichage m.** *bulletin board*

tablette f. *tablet*

talentueux/se *talented*

tapis m. *rug*

tasse f. *cup* **tasse de café** *cup of coffee*

téléphone m. *telephone*

téléspectateur/trice m./f. *TV viewer*

télévision f. *television*

terminer *to finish, end*

terrain de sport m. *sports field*

terrasse f. *patio, deck, terrace*

thé m. *tea*

théâtre m. *theater*

tiroir m. *drawer*

toi *you*

toilettes f. pl. *restroom*

toit m. *roof*

ton, ta, tes *your*

toucher *to touch*

toujours *always*

tourner *to turn*

tout droit *straight ahead*

tout le temps *all the time*

transporter *to transport*

travail m. *work*

travailler *to work*

travailleur/se *hardworking*

trombone m. *paperclip*

trottoir m. *sidewalk*

trouver *to find*

tu *you*

typique *typical*

un(e) m./f. *a, an, one*

université f. *university*

usine f. *factory*

utile *useful*

utiliser *to use*

valise f. *suitcase*

vase m. *vase*

vendeur/se m./f. *salesman, saleswoman*

vendredi m. *Friday, on Friday* **le vendredi** *on Fridays*

venir *come* **venir de** *to have just (done something)*

verre m. *glass* **verre à vin** *wine glass* **verre de vin** *glass of wine*

vert m. (noun) *green;* **vert(e)** (adj.) *green*

vêtement m. *piece of clothing* **vêtements** m.pl. *clothes*

veuf/veuve *widowed*

viande f. *meat*

victorieux/se *victorious, winning*

vidéo f. *video*

vieillard m. *senior citizen, elderly person*

vieux/vieille *old*

ville f. *city*

viole<u>t/tte</u> *purple*

visiter *to visit*

visiteu<u>r/se</u> m./f. *visitor*

voilà…! *there's…! there are…!*

voisin(e) m./f. *neighbor*

voiture f. *car*

votre, vos *your*

vouloir *want (verb)*

vous *you*

vrai(e) *real, true*

vue f. *view*

Y a-t-il…? *Is/Are there…?*